T5-AFL-675

Stich u. Druck v Weger in Leipzig

Felix Mendelssohn Bartholdy

MY RECOLLECTIONS

OF

FELIX MENDELSSOHN-BARTHOLDY,

AND HIS LETTERS TO ME.

BY

EDUARD DEVRIENT,

OFFICIAL DIRECTOR OF THE OPERA AT CARLSRUHE.

Translated from the German,

BY

NATALIA MACFARREN.

VIENNA HOUSE
New York

ML
410
.M5
D5
1972

Originally published by Richard Bentley
London, 1869

First Vienna House edition published 1972

International Standard Book Number:
0-8443-0002-0

Library of Congress Catalogue Card Number: 72-163799

Manufactured in the United States of America

NOTE BY THE TRANSLATOR.

THE biographical notes in this work have been added in order to give an idea of the intellectual status of some of the persons with whom Mendelssohn came in contact, to such readers as may be less conversant with German celebrities than the public for which the book was written. The other notes explain themselves.

ALMA COLLEGE
MONTEITH LIBRARY
ALMA, MICHIGAN

PREFACE.

THE personal history of our great men has at all times excited deep and universal interest. The public feels, and connoisseurs know, that the artist's creations are the flower of his personality, and believe they understand those creations better when he himself is known.

Besides, a purely human sympathy causes us to search into the life and character of creative artists. In these gifted and much honoured men we think we behold the highest type of mankind; we are profoundly interested to watch how intense susceptibility and vivid intellectual life is reconciled in them with simple human nature. We do not yet possess any biography of Felix Mendelssohn - Bartholdy, embracing both his

artistic and private life; this is as well, and in
probable accordance with his wishes. I have repeatedly declined to take upon myself the honourable and friendly task of writing such a biography
when pressed by his family to do so. Meanwhile
a careful critical analysis of Mendelssohn's compositions, by Reissman, has appeared, and Felix's
brother Paul conceived the happy idea of publishing a collection of his deceased brother's letters,
which, being for the most part confidential, reveal
a glimpse of his sunny nature. But the publication
of these letters lay under manifold restrictions,
and the second collection extended to a greater
number of correspondents, and treated of business
matters. A further contribution to the knowledge
of Mendelssohn as a man, which aims at nothing
but to record the living intercourse with an intimate friend and the circumstances connected
with that intercourse, may at this time not prove
unacceptable.

As regards Mendelssohn as a musician, his
works speak for him; and of these I shall only

note some occasional impressions; but much that was shared between us during twenty-six of Mendelssohn's thirty-eight years, will throw light upon his artistic career, and lead to a clearer knowledge of his lovable and finely-strung nature,—noble even in its weaknesses and short-comings.

THE AUTHOR.

CARLSRUHE, July, 1868.

NOTE.—It may be interesting here to add the inscription on Mendelssohn's tombstone, as it was read by Mr. C. L. Grun-eisen in November last:

Jacob Ludwig Mendelssohn-Bartholdy,
Geboren zu Hamburg am 3 Feb. 1809,
Gestorben zu Leipzig am 4 November 1847.

Whence the name by which he is endeared to the world, and which so fitly describes him, "Felix," has not been told. The neglected state in which Mr. Gruneisen found the great musician's grave, is mournful to read of.—TR.

MY RECOLLECTIONS OF

FELIX MENDELSSOHN-BARTHOLDY,

AND HIS LETTERS TO ME.

WHEN I first became personally acquainted with Felix Mendelssohn, in January, 1822, he was a boy of scarcely thirteen years old, I a young man of more than twenty. I had been engaged as baritone at the Royal Opera in Berlin nearly three years, and my character had received stability from an early betrothal.

It was six years since the Mendelssohn family had quitted Paris and removed to Berlin; originally they had lived in Hamburg, where Felix was born, February 3, 1809. I had seen the boy occasionally,—his long brown curls had attracted my notice as he trudged sturdily through the streets in his big shoes, holding his father's

B

hand. Of late years I had often noticed him, when on my accustomed way to my betrothed, busily playing at marbles or touchwood with other boys before the door of his grandmother's house on the new Promenade. I had heard in musical circles of the extraordinary talents of the boy, had seen him at the Singakademie,* at Zelter's † Friday practices, and had met him at a musical party, where he took his place amongst the grown-up people, in his child's dress—a tight-fitting jacket, cut very low at the neck, and over which the wide trousers were buttoned ; into the slant-ing pockets of these the little fellow liked to thrust his hands, rocking his curly head from side to side, and shifting restlessly from one foot to the other. With half-closed eyelids, beneath which

---

* The Singakademie is a long-established and admirable society for the practice more especially of sacred music. After the death of its founder Fasch, (in the employ of Frederick the Great), Zelter became conductor, which post he held till his death in 1832.—Tr.

† Zelter has a claim to the grateful remembrance of all lovers of musical art. Himself a master of theory, and composer for the Church, the teacher of Mendelssohn, and friend of Goethe, he was the first promoter of the faith and study of Sebastian Bach, upon which the great German musicians of the last two generations have built themselves.—Tr.

flashed his bright brown eyes, he would almost
defiantly, and with a slight lisp, jerk out his
answers to the inquisitive and searching questions
that people usually address to young prodigies.
His technical command of the pianoforte, and
musicianly way of playing, struck me then as
surprising, but still inferior to that of his elder
sister Fanny, and compositions, even little
operas of the child, were talked of. My betrothed, Theresa, had meanwhile become acquainted with Fanny at the Singakademie, and
as it was intended this winter to renew the trials of
Felix's operatic compositions at the Mendelssohns'
house, Zelter proposed her as soprano, and thus
she was introduced. My turn soon came. The
Concertmeister Henning—Felix's violin teacher
—who was to have sung the bass, found himself
unable to do so, and proposed me as his substi-
tute. Thus I came to be concerned in the performances of Felix's first operas at his parents'
house.

Considering the wealth ascribed to Felix's
father, the house gave an impression of studied
plainness : the walls and furniture were of extreme

simplicity, but the drawing-room was decorated with engravings of the Loggie of Raphael. The singers sat round the large dining-table, and close to the grand piano, raised on a high cushion, sat Felix, grave and unembarrassed, leading and directing us with an ardour as if it had been a game he was playing with his comrades.

That so many grown people should be troubling themselves about compositions of his, seemed to impress him much less than that this was his second operetta, and that he was actually engaged upon a third. He was there for the sole purpose of hearing and performing the music, and he took for granted that it was the same with us. It struck us the very first evening how weak self-consciousness and vanity were in his nature, in comparison with emulation, and the determination of thoroughly mastering whatever he undertook. When the little work had been tried through, his first thought was carefully to collect the parts and place them in order; this he did before he would take any notice of our admiring comments on the work. These he received pleasantly enough, but preferred to lead off the conversation to questions or explanations on the details of performance.

There were two one-act operas which we rehearsed several times, "Die beiden Pedagogen" (the two schoolmasters)—which had already been tried, together with his first attempt, "Soldaten Liebschaft," unknown to me—and a new one, "Die wandernden Virtuosen" (the wandering minstrels). The librettos of these were put together, from French *vaudevilles*, by young Doctor Caspar.* The music was individual, the declamation of the words unsought and natural; there were no striking melodies, but the comic incidents were treated with skill and humour. I tried to find reminiscences of former composers, but at most was slightly reminded of Dittersdorf.† In the second opera a duet between a pretended and a real schoolmaster, who disputed about the respective systems of Badesow and Pestalozzi, was most effective. Doctor Caspar and I sang it,

* Afterwards consulting physician.

† A Viennese, a very popular composer of comic operas at the end of the last century. One of these, "The Doctor and the Apothecary," may still be heard occasionally in Germany. —Tr.

to general amusement, at rehearsals and at a large party.

From this time forth Theresa and I became familiar in the Mendelssohns' house : Felix liked me, the parents approved, and Theresa and Fanny became more and more intimate. We now had many musical evenings, some readings of Shakspeare's plays, each one taking a part; and were present, either as listeners or executants, at the Sunday performances, to which the wealthy father was able to assemble a small orchestra selected from the court-band—so that Felix enjoyed the inestimable advantage of becoming acquainted with the nature and treatment of the different instruments already in his boyish years, and of hearing his own compositions with the instruments for which they were written. On these occasions he used to stand on a stool before his music-desk, and look amongst the sedate musicians, especially near the giant double-bass, a wonder-child indeed, in his boy's suit, shaking back his long curls, and looking over the heads of the musicians like a little general; then stoutly waving his *bâton*, firmly and quietly conducted his piece to the end, meanwhile noting and listening to every little detail as it passed.

Of course other compositions besides his own were given at these Sunday performances, and both he and Fanny played trios, and concerted pieces with the orchestra. The effect of this early initiation into the knowledge of the orchestra, and into the routine of conducting, is self-evident. I had opportunity to notice the rich stores of learning and powerful influences that were brought to bear upon his education. The mother first perceived the musical talent of the two eldest children, and began to teach them. In Berlin they were placed under the excellent but crusty Zelter, for thorough bass; under the genial, tender-hearted Berger,* for pianoforte; and under the accurate Henning, for violin. The droll little Professor Rösel taught them landscape-drawing: Felix profited more from him than his sisters, he learnt to free himself from his master's manner-

---

* A pupil of Clementi, and long a teacher and composer in Berlin. His studies are well known to thoughtful players. Schumann esteemed him highly. He was also master of W. Taubert.—Tr.

isms. The young Doctor Heyse * was tutor to
the four children, all of extraordinary capacity;
his quiet thoroughness guided Felix's scholastic
studies until he was prepared for the University
examination. His younger sister, Rebecca, shared
the lessons in Greek with Felix, in order to make
the study more attractive to him. The mother,
a highly-cultivated and intelligent woman as
well as an active housewife, ever occupied either
in reading or some domestic duty, kept the children to their work with inflexible energy. The
unceasing activity of Felix, which became a necessity of life with him, is no doubt to be ascribed
to early habit. He must have often wearied of
his tasks at the mother's feet, by Rebecca's little
table. If I called in the forenoon upon the
mother, and he came with his lunch into the
front room, during which he was allowed to
quit his work, and we happened to chat longer

* It is worthy of remark, in enumerating the many happy
influences that were brought to bear upon the gifted boy, that
this Dr. Heyse was son of the celebrated grammarian, and,
later, the father of the esteemed poet, Paul Heyse, author of
the popular "Novellen." This "young Dr. Heyse" was a
distinguished philologist and teacher.—Tr.

than the bread-and-butter rendered necessary, the mother's curt exclamation, " Felix, are you doing nothing ?" quickly drove him away into the back room.

But it was easy to perceive that the most important influence upon the son's development was the father. Abraham Mendelssohn was a remarkable man, in whose mental and spiritual being life was reflected with singular clearness. His thoughts and feelings led him to find the highest satisfactions in the intellect. This was natural in the Jewish-born son of the philosopher Moses Mendelssohn, but to me, then in the age of religious effervescence, this did not become clear till later in life, and by degrees; his sound and certain judgment, however, impressed me even then. The conviction that our life is given us for work, for usefulness, and constant striving —this conviction Felix inherited from his father. Abraham Mendelssohn's contentious disposition, which increased with his years and became more and more acrid, and at last intolerable, is strangely anomalous with so much wisdom, and may have arisen from physical causes. Had this excessive irritability anything to do with his sudden death, and was it to descend upon Felix?

When we add, to the enumeration of the many distinguished talents that helped in his education, the influence of family friends, both old and young, and of many remarkable strangers who visited at the house, we may assert, that of all the famous Germans, none had so favoured a youth as Felix Mendelssohn.

Meanwhile the summer of 1822 had arrived, and whilst the entire Mendelssohn family were preparing for an extensive tour in Switzerland, I set out on a journey to complete my studies; which, taking me through Dresden and up the Rhine, led me to remain some time at Frankfort-on-the-Main. There in the street I met one day Dr. Heyse and Felix, whose appearance was much changed; the pretty brown curls were cut short to the neck, the child's dress had given place to the boy's suit,—an open jacket over a waistcoat. The alteration was suited to his age, but I could not but regret his former unique appearance.

The family, now on their way home, had broken their journey for a few days at Frankfort, during which time I was their constant guest. Here the young Ferdinand Hiller, a few years younger than Felix, also a boy with long brown curls, was introduced by his father, and this was the beginning of a lasting friendship. The music-seller and composer, André of Offenbach, a stout man, with loud speech and noisy laugh, came also to make acquaintance with Felix, and showed some of his new songs. He requested Felix to extemporize on the piano, an art that, since the precedent of Hummel, was much thought of and looked upon as the true test of a first-rate pianist and musician,— Felix, who had already given tokens of remarkable power for this task, had a quiet bit of fun on this occasion. He ingeniously wove an air of André, that had just been sung, into his improvisation, together with one of my humble attempts, that had lain in his all-retaining memory, though I had only shown it to him once, and elaborated them. He laughed about it afterwards, and recalled with much amusement how the big André, sitting close to the piano, greeted his air at each recurrence with a loud chuckle, whilst I, standing behind Felix's chair, acknowledged my little theme with a gentle purr, and how he made us repeat these accomplishments again and again. But at the Cecilia Society, where Felix also extemporized, at the request of the Director Schelble, he treated the matter more seriously. Taking his subjects from the motets of Bach that had just been sung, he fairly amazed all hearers by his wealth of invention, his complete command of counterpoint, as well as by his astounding execution and sustained energy. This hour secured for the boy Schelble's friendship, and convinced me of his great vocation.

Returned to Berlin, our intercourse with the Mendelssohns' house grew yet closer: Theresa became intimate with Fanny, and the depositary of her growing inclination towards the painter, Hensel, likewise my friend. This latter also confided to me his love for Fanny, and the obstacles opposed to it by the mother on account of his tendency to Roman Catholicism, which was just then in vogue at Berlin, and thus we were united by a kind of sympathetic chain,—the lovers, Theresa and I,—although, of course, we two abstained from every kind of interference. In the summer of 1823, when I went to Vienna to study under the famous company of Italian singers, with Lablache at their head, then performing there, we met again, by agreement; Hensel was on his way to Rome, and the sympathetic chain was continued through my correspondence with Theresa.

Meanwhile Felix was steadily progressing with his studies and compositions. Not less valuable for his experience than the orchestral performances (which were repeated from time to time on Sunday mornings) were, in another direction, the Friday practices at Zelter's. At these were assembled a select number of the members of the Singakademie, who were desirous to know the difficult works of the old masters. Here we used to sing what Zelter called the " bristly pieces " of Sebastian Bach, who was at that time generally considered as an unintelligible musical arithmetician, with an astonishing facility in writing fugues; few of his motets were sung by the society, and these but seldom.

As Zelter's pupil, I was drawn into the Friday practices at his house soon after my entering the Singakademie (1818). I there met Felix and Fanny, who sang alto in the chorus; both had been occasionally called upon to accompany at the piano, but henceforth this task devolved upon Felix alone.

Thus he became acquainted with musical works, which Zelter kept hidden as a mysterious sacred treasure from the world, which he supposed no longer capable of prizing it. Here, too, Felix heard a few pieces from Bach's " Passions-Musik " for the first time, and it became his ardent longing to possess a copy of the great Passion according to the Gospel of St. Matthew: this longing was fulfilled by his grandmother on Christmas, 1823. It had not been easy to obtain permission from Zelter to transcribe it, who was a jealous collector; the transcription was undertaken by Eduard Rietz, an excellent young violinist, of a delicate and sensitive organisation, who had replaced Henning as violin master to Felix, and in whom the young pupil confided with the full ardour of a first friendship. On

Christmas Day, when Theresa and I were invited there, Felix, with a countenance beaming with reverence and joy, showed me the admirably written copy of the sacred masterpiece, which was now to form his favourite study.

In the following year, 1824, besides some instrumental compositions, Felix had completed a comic opera in three acts, "Der Onkel aus Boston;" the libretto was again by Dr. Caspar. Theresa and I assisted at a series of amusing rehearsals of this work, and at two performances of the music, the dialogue being read between the pieces. This work, in comparison with his first operettas, gave manifest tokens of progress in the command of melody and in vocal part-writing. A trio between tenor and two sopranos, and an aria for soprano were conspicuous instances of this; but the happiest effect in the work was a congratulatory chorus for female voices with solo: this some zealous friends somewhat indiscreetly compared with the bridesmaids' chorus in "Der Freischütz," then in the first flush of its popularity. Ludwig Robert, who had followed

the Varnhagens to Berlin, and who was intimate
in the Mendelssohns' house, proposed to write a
libretto for Felix, in which this piece was to form
the central idea, recurring again and again
throughout the work. The parents, however, had
too much sense to consent to such a thing.

A few days after the performance of this opera
I was married to Theresa, amidst the kindest con-
gratulations of the Mendelssohns. This event, to
some extent, estranged Felix from me for a time.
The youth of fifteen found much that was changed
in me through my present position: he felt a
kind of deference for me as the head of a household, and a delicate shyness towards the associate
of a female being. As young married people are
wont to isolate themselves, it happened that about
this time we visited the family less frequently
than hitherto, and I heard little of Felix's doings.
I was fully aware, however, of the manifold influences that were working out his development.
The then pleasant institution in Berlin of un-
ceremonious evening calls, with the plainest entertainment, prevailed to perfection in the Mendelssohns' house, and gave rise to the most uncon-

strained and suggestive intellectual intercourse. Amongst the uninvited and ever-welcome guests there were, Dr. Caspar, always full of life and spirits, and his merry young wife; the young Secretary of the Hanoverian Legation, Klinge-mann, son of the professor, manager, and author, August Klingemann, a gentlemanly man, whose somewhat formal demeanor concealed a sympathetic nature, which Felix fully understood, for it became the foundation of the warmest friendship. He was mostly accompanied by Dr. Hermann Frank, quite a contrast to Klingemann, of cool and decided bearing, self-reliant in thought and deed; he was a *littérateur*, as far as was compatible with the then existing censorship for one who loved to utter pungent truths, without considering the consequences. He argued much with Felix's father, and cared nothing for the son's music. Then there were Ludwig Robert,* the witty and intellectual writer, and his handsome wife, who wrote pretty verses, and always brought sunshine with her; Robert's sister, too,

---

* Poet, dramatist and satirist, author of " Die Macht der Verhängnisse."—TR.

the celebrated Rahel, and her husband, Varnhagen,* who had begun to pay the penalty of his imprudent liberalism by a life of enforced idleness at Berlin. In this circle Felix heard much that awoke and stimulated thought. Foreign musicians mostly brought introductions to the house, and afforded endless entertainment and suggestions to Felix and Fanny. One of these was the strange and talented violinist Boucher, who bore an extraordinary resemblance to Napoleon I., and was quite a curiosity to the Mendelssohns. He traded on his Bonaparte profile by putting his violin aside during the *tuttis* of the orchestra and exhibiting himself in the well-known imperial attitudes. Sometimes he would play holding his

---

* This remarkable man, of ancient descent, distinguished himself as poet, novelist, soldier, and diplomatist. In 1804 he published a "Musenalmanach" with Chamisso. He was wounded at Wagram under Austrian colours; in 1813 he commanded a Russian regiment, and in 1814 attended the Congress of Vienna. The political reaction in Germany of 1819 put an end to his public career. His biographical works, criticisms, and memoirs are numerous. Rahel Levin, his wife, shared the studies of his compulsory retirement. Some of her letters have been published, and she has been called a "female Hamlet." Varnhagen died in 1858. His correspondence with Alexander v. Humboldt was published after his death.—Tr.

violin behind his back ; these tricks, together
with his occasional really fine playing, brought
him a series of exceptionally crowded rooms.
He was an extraordinary mixture of *naïveté*, cra-
ziness, and a French adroitness in turning everything to profit.   There were also the flutist
Guillot, whose dashing execution overstepped
the limits of his instrument, and the measured
Drouet, who, on the other hand, combined extreme softness of tone with the utmost fluency of
execution.   Then there was Moscheles, much
looked up to by Felix, and Reissiger, before his
promotion to the post of Kapellmeister in Dresden.   It could not be but that Felix should receive the most varied and stirring impressions
from coming in contact with so many different
types of power and character.

I had at this time become so convinced that it
was Felix's vocation to devote himself to dramatic music of the highest stamp, that I tried
my inexperienced pen on a libretto, for the subject of which I chose the episode of Olind and
Sophronia, from the " Jerusalem Delivered " of
Tasso; this had been a favourite with me since

my Italian studies. I read my piece to Felix and Heyse in November, 1824; they praised it, but Felix thought he would not yet like to venture on a subject so grave, and so the attempt remained unused. At the time I was not aware that Felix had been at work on a new opera since July, and he, probably, did not like to tell me this at the moment. Klingemann had furnished the libretto for him this time; the subject was " Camacho's Wedding," from Cervantes' " Don Quixote." This work he completed in August, 1825. With this composition, and with the removal of the family from the grandmother's house in the new Promenade, Felix's boyhood closes. The father had bought the so-called " Reck'sche Palais" in the Leipziger Strasse, and after some building alterations the family moved into it towards the end of the summer, 1825.

In the new house Felix entered upon his young manhood, with freshly awakened powers and inclinations. With his usual energy and ardour he now devoted himself to gymnastic exercises. The father had a small gymnasium fitted up for his

sons in the large and beautiful garden of the house.
Felix attained the greatest perfection in these
exercises, and was able to keep them up for a
long time. He took great pleasure, too, in his
riding-lessons, and used to have much to tell about
the horses, and of the jokes of the old royal riding-
master, which I already knew. Swimming was
practised during the ensuing summer with intense enjoyment. A small swimming society
had been formed; Klingemann, who lived at the
Hanoverian Embassy, which was in an upper
story of the Mendelssohns' house, belonged to this
society; he wrote the words of swimming-songs,
to which Felix composed the music, and these
the members tried to sing as they were swimming
about; endless merriment grew out of this, and
at the supper-table there was enough to recount
of youthful pranks and freaks. Klingemann, who
was soon afterwards removed to the embassy in
London, grew more and more intimate with
Felix; he aroused his and Fanny's sympathy in
Jean Paul, whose infinite tenderness and profound sense of humour exercised great influence
on Felix. They were kindred natures. His

musical career was now pursued publicly and in good earnest; the elder Mendelssohn, to satisfy himself of Felix's thorough competency, took him to Paris in the autumn of 1825, to consult Cherubini, who, after reading through some of his compositions and hearing a pianoforte concerto and a string quartet, congratulated the youth on his great promise. Subsequently Felix had an opportunity of playing Beethoven's Fantasia* at a concert given by Maurer, the violinist, where also was performed his last composition, the overture in C. We gave it the name of trumpet overture, because of the frequently recurring trumpet-call. It was again played at the Sunday performances at the Mendelssohns' house, which were now regular institutions, and later, in 1833, at the musical festival at Düsseldorf; moreover, the father of Felix was so fond of this overture, that I have heard him say he would like to hear it in his dying hour. Notwithstanding all this, Felix did not look upon it as fit for publication. He made no scruple, therefore, afterwards to introduce this

* It is to be supposed that the Choral Fantasia is meant. —Tr.

trumpet-call in his later overture, "The Isles of
Fingal."

And now a public trial was to be made of
his operatic talent. Motherly fondness yearned
to witness the son's great success: "Camacho's
Wedding," after several alterations, was declared
to be finished. It was sent in to the royal
theatre in 1826; the General Director, Count
Brühl, expressed himself kindly disposed towards
the maiden effort of the young composer, but
Spontini, who, as chief musical director, had the
casting vote in the acceptance of operas, was inimical to everything that could have a chance of
public favour. He took every occasion of asserting
his own merits and importance, and of making his
official consequence felt. Spontini demanded the
score for perusal before he delivered judgment.
Dignity required that the examination should
last some time; it might have lasted still longer
had he really read the score, for this was by no
means his forte. At last the young musician was
summoned: the score was criticised with pitying
depreciation, winding up with the following ad-
monition,—as Spontini led the young man to

the window, which was opposite to the dome of the Jewish church,—"Mon ami, il vous faut des idées grandes, grandes comme cette coupole."

The opera, however, was to be produced; but other works claimed precedence, and hindrances innumerable were raised; so that the elder Mendelssohn, who had known Spontini in Paris, had frequently met him and received him at his house, had angry words about it, which ended in a total estrangement.

Through the mediation of Count Brühl, the parts of the opera were at last given out, at the beginning of 1827, to go through the usual snail's-pace routine that then prevailed in operatic matters.

Until then I had only heard single pieces from the "Wedding of Camacho" on the piano. I knew the libretto, and entertained grave doubts as to its being in any respect more important than "Der Onkel aus Boston," or, in fact, of sufficient weight to be the framework for Felix's first step into the public world. I sang the part of Carrasco at all the rehearsals, and gradually my doubts became certainties.

The plot of the opera, already popular in the
"Dorfbarbier,"* is only suited for a comic dé-
nouement. The pretended poisoning of the rejected
lover, his sudden restoration the instant the marriage is effected, must always produce a laughable
effect. In the "Dorfbarbier," the verdict that the
universal panacea is "Schinken" (ham) closes the
action more in the spirit of the plot than does, in
the "Wedding of Camacho," the interference of
Don Quixote. Besides, the inherent deficiencies
of the plot, the poet's inadequacy to develop
dramatic situations and effects, was paralyzing to
the composer. Don Quixote and Sancho Panza
scarcely entered into the action of the piece.

The music was essentially of the same character
as all Felix's boyish works. The hearer was at
once struck by the admirable musicianship, command of form, and intelligent declamation of the
vocal parts ; these qualities were indisputable and
claimed esteem for the young composer of sixteen,
but they alone would not command success with
the public. The skill with which the comic in-

* A comic opera by J. Schenk, that had been popular for
more than thirty-five years.—Tr.

cidents were turned to account did not exceed that of his boyish operettas; in invention the work was poor; in melodies worth preserving I thought it inferior to the " Onkel," inasmuch as that during the entire course of the rehearsals I had not grown attached to a single melody, which I certainly had to several in the previous work. Felix afterwards inserted a song from " Camacho's Wedding," in his second book of songs,* but it has not become a favourite, and clearly shows the then immature condition of its composer's power for passionate expression. It was not then appropriate to utter these opinions; one point, however, I warmly contested with Felix, because he set store by it, and this was the musical treatment of the character of Don Quixote. Throughout the opera, every speech of the Don, bearing upon his boastful knighthood, was ushered in by an imposing flourish of trumpets; no real hero could have been announced with greater dignity. But here, where the intention was to characterise a crazy knight-errant (however loyal in his self-

* With the words " Einmal aus seinen Blicken." No. 10 of the English edition.—Tr.

imposed mission), I thought he ought to have chosen such instrumentation as would convey an ironical sense of knight-errantry.* Felix, on the contrary, maintained that the knight of the rueful countenance believed himself to be a genuine hero, capable of all glorious deeds, and that the composer ought to express the feelings of his dramatic personage, not his own. In answer to this, I drew his attention to the fact that Cervantes himself everywhere places the grotesqueness of antiquated chivalry in the strongest light; I urged that the composer might safely follow the poet, and that no actor would think of personating the old knight as a veritable hero, but always as the vainglorious boaster; and how was this universal interpretation of the character to be reconciled with the grandiose instrumentation of Felix?

This fertile subject was much discussed; I was surprised to find that Felix's father took his son's view of the matter; this was, probably, because it was now beyond recall.

---

* Felix has something of the same kind in the " Midsummer-Night's Dream," in the flourish at the " Hail, hail!" of Peasblossom, Cobweb, Moth, and Mustard-seed.

The opera had now to pass through the usual intrigues and delays of theatres. Just as we were ready for the stage rehearsals, Blum, who was to have sung Don Quixote, was taken ill with jaundice, and the doctor prescribed change of air and cessation of work. It was now a question, whether the rehearsals should be suspended and the opera postponed for four or six weeks, so that Blum should be well enough to resume his part : for the success of the work this would have been best. But we were all impatient. What new obstacles might not arise ? Blum pledged himself to perform to the end of his stay in town, in spite of illness, which would make two performances possible ; these we resolved to have. Even at the last moment difficulties sprang up ; the chorus-master protesting that the chorus could not be sure of their parts by the day fixed for the first performance : the liberality of the father surmounted this objection ; still between managers and artists the date of production was deferred until the very end of Blum's stay, the 29th of April, which cut off all possibility of an immediate repetition. The performance was not to

take place at the opera-house, but at the theatre.
Felix preferred the smaller building as better
suited to the character of the work. The house
was crowded with well-wishers, and the applause
was profuse and enthusiastic ; the music, however,
did not give genuine pleasure. The young composer, too, must have felt this. The work represented his musical thought of two years ago ; he
had now outgrown it and felt so doubtful amidst
the applause of his friends that he quitted the
theatre before the end of the performance, and
when called before the curtain, I had to make an
apology for him.

Whilst the family rejoiced in the apparent success, Felix remained annoyed and dissatisfied;
he said nothing, however. When Blum was con-
valescent, new objections arose ; the managing
powers neglected the matter, and when Felix
was at last applied to about the repetition of his
opera, he answered testily " that it was the manager's business to see about it, not his." After
this the matter was allowed to drop.

A spiteful criticism, though it appeared in no
better journal than Saphir's *Schnellpost*, also

wounded Felix. Even then he felt, what in later days he often confessed to me, that the most brilliant praise of the best journal has not so much power to gratify, as the contemptible abuse of the most obscure paper has to vex. Moreover, he learnt that the abusive article was written by a highly-gifted musical student, who had been hospitably received by Mendelssohn's father, who had witnessed and shared the excitement of the family during the preparation of the opera, and who knew the score well.

This chain of annoyances was unconsciously the foundation of Felix's repugnance to Berlin. Later, when these excitements had subsided, I asked him if he did not think the construction of the opera had had some share in the exceptionally adverse fate that had pursued it? He half assented, but concluded by saying, " the opera was not bad enough to deserve such very scurvy treatment." And in this I quite agreed with him.

These events, however, were not destined to weigh down Felix's creative powers,—from this moment they took a higher flight. He now wrote his overture to the " Midsummer-Night's Dream."* When Moscheles came to Berlin, in November, it was finished, and he and Fanny played it to us, arranged for four hands.

This work is clearly the bright turning-point in Felix's career as a composer. He here throws off scholastic fetters and stands forth in native strength. Such a rendering in music of the characteristic features of a poetical masterpiece, marks the immense stride he had made. His previous dramatic attempts were conceived with correctness and intelligence; but here the intention is striking and unmistakeable, and irresistibly fascinating. The Mendelssohn we possess and cherish, dates from this composition.

* As to Mendelssohn we owe the origination of such characteristic pieces for the orchestra as the above, the " Calm Sea and Prosperous Voyage," " Isles of Fingal," and " Melusine," it is a pity he did not give to them a fitter title than " Overtures." " Fantasias for the Orchestra" they might more aptly be called. He was more happy in entitling his " songs without words," which bygone writers would have simply called " études." (Herr Devrient overlooks that the " overture" form is strictly adhered to in the above works, which in form and purpose can scarcely be called innovations, when we bear in mind Beethoven's " Leonora," " Coriolan," and " Egmont" overtures.—TR.)

After repeatedly hearing the work for four hands, then, in the large drawing-room, with full orchestra (which for the first time brought to light its richness of colouring), all friends recognized the eventful nature of this work. The picturesqueness, sentiment, poetic beauty, refinement, and engaging mirthfulness of Felix's nature were all here set forth ; all qualities that pointed to the dramatic, characteristic branch of musical art for their proper field of action,* His father also felt that his genius was now self-existent, and that further teaching would only fetter him. The lessons with Zelter were therefore discontinued, which somewhat irritated the old gentleman, who considered that Felix had learnt everything from him, and had not yet outgrown his leadership.

Marx, who had lately become intimate at Mendelssohn's, used to say that Zelter had seen

---

* Every one will sympathise with the above enthusiastic tribute; the substance of it, however, should be received with some reserve. The octet had been written in the previous year, which, for fire and originality, Mendelssohn never surpassed; also the quintet in A, Op. 18, in the first three movements of which the true Mendelssohnian idiom already breaks itself way.—Tr.

the fish swim, and imagined he had shown him how. But the affectionate nature of Felix was grieved at his old teacher's vexation, and sought to assuage it by increased devotion and regard.

There were now several accessions to the intimate frequenters of the house ; young men, who though several years older than Felix, were, owing to his advanced culture and development, on an equal footing with himself. He attended the University of Berlin in 1827 and 1828, where Heyse was now appointed professor, and consequently no longer sojourned with the Mendelssohns. Instead of the usual essay, Felix had sent in a translation of Terence's "Maid of Andros." * He attended the courses of several professors, according to his own choice, and had a particular predilection for Ritter's geographical lectures. Some University friends now visited the house ; amongst them were Droysen,† at this

---

* It was published in Berlin by Dümmler, without Felix's name, with an introduction and remarks by Heyse. The MS. was presented to me later by his widow, as a remembrance of Felix.

† A distinguished classical scholar and historian.—Tr.

time a divinity student, who wrote verses, which
Felix and Fanny delighted to set to music; the
brothers Heydemann, one a lawyer, the other a
philologist; Dorn,* who abandoned science for
the sake of music; Kugler, † who was at that
time half student, half painter; Schubring, a
theological student, with whom I was on friendly
terms; my cousin and friend Baur,‡ whom I had
introduced at the Mendelssohns' musical parties,
and who, having been a first-class man in 1813,
was able to give some valuable hints to Felix;
both were disciples of Schleiermacher. They
sang lustily whatever Felix gave out for practice,
assisted him afterwards in his oratorios, and remained his faithful friends till the close of his
life. Eduard Rietz was Felix's constant especial
confidant, initiated in all his musical doings: this

* Now conductor at the Royal Chapel in Berlin. (Dorn had
the honour of giving lessons in composition to Schumann;
some of the latter's letters and criticisms attest the spirit in
which these lessons were given and received.—TR.)

† A man of universal culture, poet, historian, but more
popularly known as an art critic, through his admirable
"Handbook of Painting." Died in 1858.—TR.

‡ A copious writer on divinity, the first in Germany to set
forth the progressive nature of true Christianity.—TR.

companionship did not, however, extend to the drawing-room, where Rietz seldom appeared; partly through love of solitude, and partly through his increasing chest disease. Klingemann now was gone, and Marx, a frequent visitor, was made much of. His intellectual and flowing speech dominated every conversation, his many new and striking ideas, his adroit flattery, so discreetly veiled, made him, for a time, very popular with the family, notwithstanding his awkward manners, his ungainly appearance, short trousers, and clumsy shoes. The father Mendelssohn alone held aloof from him.

Marx* gained an ascendency over Felix such as no one ever exercised over him. There is no doubt he had a share in the astonishing impetus Mendelssohn's powers revealed in the "Midsummer-Night's Dream." He caused the first sketch of the composition to be rejected, and urged him to a more consistent development of the leading thoughts,—in this he was verifying his musical

* Marx is better known as a critic and theorist than as a producing musician, though he has composed much. He was Professor and Doctor of Music at the Berlin University. Died about a year ago.—TR.

principles,—in short, Felix clung to him with implicit trust and affection.

A large circle of friends now used to assemble on Sunday evenings; during the summer dispersing themselves from the open drawing-room over the park-like garden, and the many blooming young friends of the daughters of the house gave Felix his first experiences in love-making. As at the winter meetings, instrumental and vocal music were the social bond. The Roberts were still in Berlin, and resided in the garden-wing of the Mendelssohns' house. Rahel often enlivened the circle. In appearance and address plain and natural, speaking at all times frankly what her ready insight and warm feelings suggested, she yet was fully aware that her sayings were noted, and by no one more than by her husband.

It could not escape observation that Varnhagen was ever watching her; even when he was at a distance he would approach when any laughter or sounds of approbation came from the quarter where she was, and ask, "What did she say then?" The future recorder of her sayings was plainly visible. Thus there was a halo of self-consciousness about this couple which made Felix uncomfortable. He never could bear celebrated women, who sit on a tripod and send their oracles abroad; Bettina, too, failed to enlist his sympathy. On the other hand, he greatly reverenced another much-talked-of lady, the wife of the Councillor Herz, for her self-denying activity in promoting the education of young girls.

Another great leader of talk was Professor Gans, especially on political subjects. In spite of his loud, broad speech, there was so much directness, kindness, and justice in what he said, that Felix could not but like him. The Steffens, too, were intimate in the house, and his honest eloquence raised the tone of conversation. Amongst the casual visitors Lindblad, the thoughtful Swedish composer; the restless Holtei, the Falstaffian and yet elegant Schall, and Heine, whose listless, *blasé* manners were far from pleasing, were remarkable to me. When the young people of the house made some enthusiastic remark about Jean Paul, he drawled out, "What of Jean Paul? he never saw the ocean."* Fanny, with ready wit, retorted, "Certainly not, he had no Uncle Solomon to pay his expenses." †

The skilful centre of this circle, composed of such manifold elements, was Felix's mother. Without ever appearing to lead, she always knew when to stimulate or check the conversation, or turn it into a new channel; this rare gift she may have acquired in Paris.

How profoundly this intellectual and refined home circle must have influenced the impressible nature of Felix!

But the social intercourse of the house received yet another stimulant when, besides the usual Sunday performances, Felix began, in the winter of 1827, to assemble a small and trusty choir, who met usually on Saturdays, for the practice of rarely-heard works. We soon entered upon his revered "Matthäus Passion." With this work a new world opened to us, as we mastered it piece by piece. The miscellaneous performance of single numbers at Zelter's did not result in a

* Heine's " Meerbilder " had just appeared.
† The rich Solomon Heine kept his nephew well supplied.

comprehension of the work as a whole. The impersonation of the several characters of the Gospel
by different voices struck us as being the pith of
the work, the antiquity of this practice in old
church music being long forgotten. The dramatic treatment that arose from it, the over-
whelming majesty of the choruses, above all the
wondrous declamation of the part of Christ, were
to me a new and sacred Bible-speech, and increased with every time of hearing our reverence
and astonishment at the greatness of this work.
Not Theresa only, all shared these impressions,
and Felix had no reason to complain of our lack
of zeal. He so identified himself with the work,
had mastered its difficulties so completely, and
knew with such exquisite skill and considerateness to impart, and penetrate us with, his clear
perception of its purport, that what had hitherto
been deemed mysterious complications, only for
the initiated, became to us natural and familiar.

The more I rejoiced in the unfolding of Felix's
marvellous capacity, the more I longed to see
him follow what I believed to be his true vocation—dramatic composition. Discouraged by the

unpleasant circumstances which attended "Cama-cho's Wedding," he declined every suggestion on the plea of unsuitable librettos. The non-success of his first attempt had made him fastidious for life.

About this time I lighted upon some Bohe-mian legends, on the subject of Hans Heiling, the king of the earth spirits, who turned an entire wedding procession, priest and all, into stones, still shown on the steep banks of the Eger. I considered this subject well adapted for an opera, and set to work upon my second libretto, in the hope that, in the absence of anything better, it might afford scope for the peculiar powers that Felix had lately put forth, to break new ground. I did not speak to him about it until the beginning of summer, when I had completed my part of the work, which seemed to me not without promise. He was anxious to see it, and we agreed that I should read it to him, and make the necessary comments; he begged that Marx might accom-pany him. They came to me at Pankow, a vil-lage where I was spending a second summer with my wife and family, and in our tiny garden the reading took place. Felix gave many signs of being interested; Marx, however, listened with cold attention, and I could see from the beginning that he had no sympathy with the work. His notion was that supernatural subjects, such as the "Freischütz," were henceforth exhausted, and the hopes of opera rested upon the working up of subjects from grand historical events. He was himself busy at the time on an opera, "Otto III.'s Pilgrimage to Rome, and Death," of which he had a great opinion.

Felix asked me to leave the poem with him for further consideration before deciding upon anything.

This summer brought him much work in the shape of compositions for festive occasions. In April he produced a cantata for the Dürer festival, the poem by Levezow; it was sung at the Academy, but made no impression. In September we had a smaller cantata, the poem by Rellstab, in honour of the scientific fête given by Alexander von Humboldt in the concert-room of the theatre by command of the king. This contained one pleasing piece, a tenor solo with chorus. These works for special occasions did not excite his best powers; he wrote them with rapidity, unfailing command of form and technical resources, but they are not true specimens of his genius.

Felix avoided all allusion to "Hans Heiling;" in the autumn, one day when we were chatting confidentially in his room on the *entresol*, I asked for his opinion about it, and he admitted that he found himself unable to warm to the subject, and unless he could do that the work could never become what it ought to be.

He spoke of a similarity in the subject to that of "Freischütz." He was probably quoting Marx's opinion, and thought this class of tale had better be avoided for some time to come; this we fully discussed. I defended popular legends as furnishing the best scope for music, the art best fitted to deal with the marvellous and supernatural, and rejected historical subjects, as in their very nature unmusical. Felix did not attempt a defence of Marx's point of view, he even agreed that legends were operatic subjects, but Heiling did not please him, he had no sympathy with the leading character, my verses did

not appear to him suggestive, and he returned to
his original argument, that faith in the subject
was the first condition from which a work of art
should spring, and that it was a crime to art, and
consequently to mankind, to enter upon a work
without it. What he said then he afterwards
repeated in a letter that he wrote me in 1831
from Venice,—a beautiful, idéal creed, which
however is scarcely fitted to be applied in real
life, as he was afterwards to prove.

The happiness I had pictured to myself, of
being able to help Felix in his operatic compositions, was dashed by his rejection of "Hans
Heiling." My work had been in vain, for it did
not occur to me to offer the poem to any other
musician.* I was still young enough to be highly
elated by Felix's worship of the ideal, and after in-
terchanging opinions and convictions on the highest matters, I parted from the glorious youth as
my heart's friend, the brotherly "Du" on my lips
and the despised poem in my pocket.

From this time forth I possessed his unlimited

---

* It was subsequently offered however to Marschner, and
produced in 1833, with success.—TR.

confidence and friendship, which in Felix was in-
genious in giving tokens of regard, as love itself.
In his veneration for Jean Paul he had adopted
many little words and expressions out of his
writings. One day we were discoursing on
the delightful friendship between Siebenkäs and
Leibgeber, and the simplicity of its expression,
which was such that, were they to meet again
in heaven, each would salute the other only
with "Good day, Leibgeber!" and "Good day,
Siebenkäs!" For a long time after this he used
to welcome me with, "Good day, Leibgeber!" to
which I failed not to reply in the words of the poet.

He had most exquisite ways of making
one feel his friendship—but never by high-flown
speeches — rather humorously, even funnily.
When, for instance, I had said or done anything
that he liked, or had satisfied him by my singing,
he would sometimes gently stroke my head, and
looking at me kindly, say, with indescribable
gravity, slightly drawling, with the Berlinese
accent, " *Edeward!*" In this funny way he con-
veyed tenderness, sympathy, respect and pleasure
at the tie that united us.

About this time he wrote his second descriptive overture, "The Calm Sea and Prosperous Voyage," which had almost as great a success with his admirers as the "Midsummer-Night's Dream." If in the latter he had shown his complete grasp of a perfect poem, and its realisation in music, the "Calm Sea" bore witness to his indwelling power to reproduce the impressions made by natural phenomena. The orchestral performances of the new work, in the summer drawing-room, were festive occasions for us; the violoncello solo from the "Prosperous Voyage" became a salutation amongst the younger friends. Meanwhile our vocal practices of the "Passion" of Bach continued, and raised our enthusiasm to the highest degree.

I longed more and more ardently to sing the part of "Christ" in public, and the desire to perform it became more and more universal. But all were dismayed at the insurmountable difficulties, not only in the work itself, with its double orchestra and double chorus, but also in the punctiliousness of the Academy and the discouraging attitude of Zelter. Moreover, arose the question,

how will the public receive a work so utterly
strange to them? In sacred concerts, a short
movement by Bach may have been performed
now and then as a curiosity, and received as a
piece of antiquarianism, but how would it be to
have for an entire evening nothing but Sebastian
Bach, whom the public conceived as unmelodious,
dry, and unintelligible? It seemed a rash undertaking.

Even the parents of Felix, who were nothing
loth to see so important an event as the revival of
the "Passion" inaugurated by their son, felt
doubtful as to the result. Marx hesitated, and
the old ladies of the Academy shook their heads.
Felix so utterly disbelieved that it could be done
that he replied to my entreaties, and those of the
still more zealous enthusiasts, Baur, Schubring,
and Kugler, only with jest and irony. He offered
to give a public performance on a rattle and
penny-trumpet, described the different phases
through which the undertaking would have to
pass, in the most ludicrous way, and absurdly
pictured the temerity it would be in him to attempt to move Berlin out of its time-honoured

groove, without credentials and the insignia of office. So hopeless seemed the chance of reviving this wondrous work, after having lain buried for a century, even amongst its truest worshippers.

I could not let the matter rest. One evening in January, 1829, after we had gone through the first part, Baur singing the "Evangelist" and Kugler the principal bass, and we had all gone home profoundly impressed, a sleepless night brought me counsel as to how a performance might be brought about. I waited impatiently for the late day to dawn; Theresa encouraged me, and so I set forth to see Felix. He was still asleep. I was going away, when Paul suggested that it was quite time to wake him ; so we went up, and Paul commenced the operation. I found, on this occasion, that Felix had not exaggerated what he told me about his death-like sleep. Paul took hold of him under the arms and raised him, calling out, " Wake, Felix, it is eight o'clock." He shook him, but it was some time before Felix said, dreamily, " Oh! leave off—I always said so—it is all nonsense——;" but his brother continued to

shake him and call out to him until he knew that
Felix was roused, when he let him fall back on
the pillow. At last Felix opened his eyes wide,
and, perceiving me, said in his usual pleasant
way, "Why, *Edeward*, where do you come from ?"
I now told him that I had something to say to
him. Paul took me to Felix's little workroom,
where, on the large white writing-table, his breakfast was waiting, while his coffee stood on the stove.

When he came in I told him to make a good
breakfast, and not to interrupt me too often. With
excellent humour and capital appetite he went at
it, and I now roundly told him that during the
night I had determined to have the " Passion "
publicly given, and that in the course of the next
few months, before his intended journey to England.

He laughed. " And who is going to conduct ?"
" You."

" The d—— I am ! My contribution is going
to be——"

" Leave me alone with your penny trumpets!
I am not jesting now, and have thoroughly considered the matter."

"Upon my word, you are growing solemn Well, let us hear."

My argument was, that having all of us the conviction that the "Matthew Passion" was the grandest and most important of German musical works, it was our duty to revive it to the world for general edification. As Felix made no rejoinder to this, I was free to draw the conclusion: "No living man but you can conduct its performance, and on this account you are bound to do it."

"If I were sure I could carry it through, I would!"

I now urged that in case he had any apprehensions about organizing the scheme by himself, both Zelter and the Singakademie owed me some return for my eight years' co-operation at all their concerts; this return I would now claim. Zelter should give the use of the room for the concert, and should lend his influence to persuade the society to sing in the choruses. Felix thought they would not refuse me. I went on to say that if he would not despise me for a partner, and share the responsibility with me — he being

E

sole musical director—the credit of the whole transaction would be sure ; and finally, that if we devoted the proceeds to some charitable object, all cavillers would be silenced. So I concluded my proposal, promising to take upon myself all the business cares, and to sing the part of Christ, he to conduct and revive the old buried treasure. Felix still looked thoughtful; he said : " What pleases me about the affair is that we are to do this together; that is nice, but Zelter will never give us his countenance. He has not been able to bring about a performance of the ' Passion,' and therefore believes it cannot be done."

I had more faith in Zelter's excellent sense and underlying kindness. But come what would, I was resolved to carry out my plan, and appeal direct to the Singakademie if he demurred. Felix could not bear the thought of doing anything in opposition to his dear old teacher; my assurance that it would not come to this, at last pacified him. His parents and Fanny approved. They were rejoiced that Felix, before taking his flight into the outer world, should accomplish

a great and memorable task. The father was
doubtful about Zelter's opposition, but we were of
good cheer.

Thus prepared, we set out at once for Zelter's
room, on the ground-floor of the Academy. At
the very door Felix said to me : "If he grows
abusive, I shall go. I cannot squabble with him."
"He is sure to be abusive," said I, "but I will
take the squabbling in hand myself."

We knocked. A loud, rough voice bid us come
in. We found the old giant in a thick cloud of
smoke, a long pipe in his mouth, sitting at his old
instrument with double row of keys. The quill-
pen he used in writing was in his hand, a sheet
of music-paper before him ; he wore drab-coloured
knee-breeches, thick woollen stockings, and embroidered slippers. He raised his head, with its
white hair combed back, his coarse, plebeian but
manly features turned towards us, and recog-
nizing us through his spectacles, he said kindly
in his broad accent : "Why, how is this? what
do two such fine young fellows want with me at
this early hour? Here, sit down." He led us

to a corner of the room, and sat down on a plain sofa; we took chairs.

Now I began my well-studied speech about our admiration of Bach, whom we had first learnt to prize under his guidance, and further studied at Mendelssohns'; that we felt irresistibly impelled to make a trial of the work in public, and that we desired, by his leave, to ask the Academy to co-operate with us. "Oh, yes," he said, tardily, putting up his chin as he generally did when he was particularly emphatic, "that is all very well, but now-a-days these things cannot be done quite so easily." He enlarged upon the difficulties of the work, which required resources such as existed in the Thomas Schule when Bach himself was cantor there; the necessity for a double orchestra and double chorus, and on the insufficiency of modern violin-playing for this music: all this had long been considered, and if the inherent obstacles could be so easily got over as we seemed to think, not one but all four Passions of Bach would have been already revived.

He had become excited, rose, put aside his pipe, and began walking about the room. We, too, rose; Felix pulled me by the sleeve, he thought nothing more could be done.

I retorted that we had considered the difficulties, but did not believe them to be insuperable. That Bach was to some extent familiarised, through Zelter's own excellent efforts, to whom Felix also owed his first knowledge of Bach; that I was longing to sing the part of Christ, and that we both believed our own enthusiasm would kindle that of all concerned, and that we should command success.

Zelter had become more and more irritated. He had thrown in several slighting expressions during my last speech, which caused Felix each time to pull me again by the sleeve, and now draw near to the door. At last the old gentleman broke out: "That one should have the patience to listen to all this! I can tell you that very different people have had to give up doing this very thing, and do you think that a couple of young donkeys like you will be able to accomplish it?"

This rough sally he fired off with immense energy. I could scarcely help laughing. Zelter

was in the habit of saying what he liked, and no
one was offended : we were ready to put up with
more than this for the sake of Bach, and our dear
old master. I looked round at Felix, who was
at the door holding the handle ; he beckoned me
to come away, and looked pale and hurt. I
motioned to him that we must stay, and recom-
menced my argument. I then pleaded that youth
was the time to grapple with difficulties, and that
it would reflect as much honour on him as on
ourselves if two of his pupils could bring about
this great result. My argument now began to
take visible effect; the crisis was passed. He
made yet some demurs, and speaking of the help
we hoped to get from the Academy choir, said,
" You will have nothing but misery with them !
To-day ten will come to rehearsal, and to-morrow
twenty will stop away." We laughed, and knew
that we had gained our point. Felix explained
how he intended to manage the rehearsals, at
first in the small room, and place the orchestra
under the leadership of Eduard Rietz. Zelter
objected nothing more ; at parting he said :
" Well, I will say a good word for you when the

time comes. Good luck go with you ; we shall
see what will come of it all." So we left our
capital old bear with thankful and friendly feelings. " We have won!" I cried, when we were
in the hall. " But listen," replied Felix. " Do
you know that you are a regular rascal, an arch-
jesuit ?" " Anything you like for the honour of
Sebastian Bach !" and triumphantly I stepped
out into the keen winter air.

Now everything went smoothly ; obstacles
vanish like ghosts when you approach them.
The principals of the Academy consented to all
we asked ; at our first choral practice twice as
many attended as at Mendelssohns', and the number increased on every occasion, and to such an
extent that the copyist could not supply parts
quickly enough. After our fifth practice we had
to remove to the large concert-room. It must be
told, however, that the many members of the
Academy, attracted by the novelty and magni-
tude of the undertaking, would, as Zelter had
foretold, scarcely have been so regular in their
attendance had they not been riveted and en-

chanted by the masterly direction of the music. Felix took the pieces of the oratorio consecutively, and exercised the chorus with inflexible exactness and full expression, so that the singers became thoroughly penetrated with the spirit of the music. His hints and explanations were clear, concise, masterly, and yet given in the most unpretending way.

Felix and I had frequent meetings to consider how the work could be shortened for performance. Giving it in its entirety was out of the question. It necessarily contained much that belonged to a former age, and what we had at heart was to convince people of its intrinsic greatness. Most of the songs would have to be omitted; of others only the symphonies could be given : the part of the Evangelist would have to be shorn of all that was not essential to the recital of the Passion. We often differed, for to us it was a matter of conscience; but what we finally determined upon seems to have been the right thing, for it has been adopted at most of the performances of the work.

It was now time to invite the solo-singers, and

we settled to make the round together. Felix was child enough to insist on our being dressed exactly alike on the occasion. We wore blue coats, white waistcoats, black neckties, black trousers, and yellow chamois-leather gloves that were then fashionable.* In this "Bach" uniform we started off gaily, after partaking of some of Felix's favourite chocolate provided by Theresa, to whom this was a solemn occasion. We were speaking of the strange chance that, just a hundred years after the work could have been last heard, it should now again see the light. "And to think," said Felix triumphantly, standing still in the middle of the Opern Platz, "that it should be an actor and a Jew that gives back to the people the greatest of Christian works."

Felix was quite carried away by his joyful mood; on other occasions he avoided all reference to his Jewish descent.

"You shall do the talking, and I will do the

* On this occasion I became aware under what strict control the young man of twenty yet stood. His pocket-money being run out, I lent him a thaler for the purchase of the gloves. His mother was displeased with me for this, saying, "One ought not to assist young people in their extravagances."

bowing," said Felix, at the first door where we had to call. We had little need of either; the four principal singers of our opera were ready and willing to help us. Their participation in the rehearsals, and the greater finish these now assumed, gave a fresh impetus to our work. Musicians and amateurs all thronged to the rehearsals, anxious to understand it better and better. All were amazed, not only at its architectonic grandeur of structure, but at its abundance of melody, its wealth of expression and of passion, at its quaint and affecting declamation, and at its dramatic power. No one had ever suspected old Bach of all this.

But Felix's share in making the splendid properties of this work felt and known is as memorable as the undertaking itself. His perfect mastery of all its details was only half his merit. His energy, perseverance, tact, and clever calculation of the resources at hand, made this masterpiece modern, intelligible, and life-like once more. Those who did not witness this, his first and greatest achievement in conductorship, can scarcely realise or appreciate the magnificent powers of

this youth of twenty. The revered presence of
Zelter gave still greater importance to the orchestral rehearsals. Until these took place, Felix had
both to accompany and to conduct, a difficult
matter with the rapid alternations of chorus and
solos in ever-changing rhythms : here he used to
play the accompaniment with the left hand, and
conduct with the right.

When we had an orchestra, the piano was
placed across the platform, between the two
choirs; it was then not yet customary for the
conductor to turn his back to the audience, except at the opera. By this means, though the
first choir was behind Felix, he faced the second
and the orchestra. This latter consisted mainly
of amateurs, only the leaders of the string and
principal wind instruments belonged to the
royal chapel. The wind instruments were placed
at the back, above the semicircular platform, and
extended towards the small concert-room through
three open doors. The task of keeping steady
this waving mass devolved upon Eduard Rietz.

Felix was as calm and collected in his difficult
post as though he had already conducted a dozen

Festivals. The quiet and simple way in which
he by a look, a movement of the head or hand,
reminded us of the inflections agreed upon, and
thus ruled every phrase; the confidence with
which he would drop his *bâton* during the longer
movements, when he knew that they were safe,
with a little nod as much as to say, "This will go
very well without me,"—listen with radiant
countenance, occasionally glancing towards me,
—in all he was as great as lovable.

We had had many discussions about the best
way of conducting. The continued beating
throughout a movement, that must necessarily
become mechanical, vexed me, and does so still.
Compositions are really whipped through sometimes by this process. It always appeared to me
that the conductor ought to beat time only when
the difficulty of certain passages, or unsteadiness
of the performers, renders it. necessary. Surely
the aim of every conductor should be to influence
without obtruding himself. Felix determined on
this occasion to show me how far this could be
done, and he succeeded to perfection.

I recall these circumstances with peculiar satisfaction, as of late years the extraordinary gesticulations of conductors have been made a feature of in musical performances.

Nothing less than the absolute success of the first resuscitation of Bach's masterpiece, on the 11th of March, 1829, could have initiated the subsequent study of this master by the leading musicians of modern times, and on this account the performance is memorable. The Academy never sang better, and whoever has heard the *ensemble* of these three to four hundred highly-trained amateurs, whoever has seen with what fervent zeal grand music can inspire them, will understand that, with the greatest of conductors, perfection was achieved.

Stümer sang the Evangelist with quiet precision, true to his *rôle* of Narrator, and without expatiating on the pathetic passages in the second part, so as to present a contrast to the acting personages. He also sang the aria "Ich will bei meinem Jesu wachen," which was too high for Bader, who, with his accustomed kindness, sang the parts of Peter and of Pilate.

The ladies, too, sang their touching music
well; the sympathetic voice of Madame Milder
in the accompanied recitative, " Du lieber Hei-
land," &c., the full voice of Fräulein von Schätzel, in the aria " Erbarme dich !" the obbligato
violin being played most expressively by Eduard
Rietz, were incomparable. So far as I was concerned, I knew that the part of Christ was the
most important of the whole work. But the
music was transcendent, the part lay well in my
voice ; I had long rehearsed it with Felix, and he
approved of my reading. Deeply affected by the
work as it proceeded, I sang with my whole soul
and voice, and believed that the thrills of devotion that ran through my veins were also felt by
the rapt hearers.

Never have I known any performance so consecrated by one united sympathy.

Our concert made an extraordinary sensation in the educated circles of Berlin. This
re-popularising of a half-forgotten master was
felt to be of pregnant import. A second performance was called for, which took place on
the 21st of March, and was crowded like the

first.* There . was yet one more, under Zelter, after Felix's departure, on Good Friday, the 17th of April, in lieu of the usual "Tod Jesu" of Graun.

All who are interested in music know how the sensation made by these performances caused other towns to make similar attempts; how the other "Passions" of Bach were taken in hand, especially that according to St. John; how attention was also turned upon the instrumental productions of the old master, how they were published, performed at concerts, &c. The worshippers of Bach, however, must not forget that the great light dawned upon them from the 11th of March, 1829, and that it was Felix Mendelssohn who gave new vitality to the most profound of composers. It is one of the dearest treasures of my life, the remembrance that I helped to spur on this great event.

Felix had now given proof of every excellence on his native soil, he was in good spirits about his projected journey to England, which was to

* The result of both concerts went towards founding a sewing school for poor girls.

prove to his father that, besides honour and applause, he could gain a livelihood by his musical powers. This the father insisted upon.

Felix had now completed his twentieth year; his productive powers had already shown that his strength lay in picturesque composition ; he was a great conductor, and his personal character was permanently fixed.

Of middle height, slender frame, and of uncommon muscular power, a capital gymnast, swimmer, walker, rider, and dancer, the leading feature of his outward and inner nature was an extraordinary sensitiveness. Excitement stimulated him to the verge of frenzy, from which he was restored only by his sound, death-like sleep. This restorative he had always at hand ; he has assured me that he had but to find himself alone and unoccupied in a room where there was a sofa, to go straightway to sleep. His brain had from childhood been taxed excessively, by the university course, study of modern languages, drawing, and much else, and to these were added the study of music in its profoundest sense. The rapidity

with which he mastered a score; his perfect understanding of the requirements of new compositions, the construction and complications of which
were at once transparent to him; his marvellous
memory, which placed under his hand the entire
range of great works; these wondrous gifts filled
me with frequent doubts as to whether his nervous power could possibly sustain him through
the length of an ordinary life.

Moreover, he would take no repose. The
habit of constant occupation, instilled by his
mother, made rest intolerable to him. To spend
any time in mere talk caused him to look frequently at his watch, by which he often gave
offence; his impatience was only pacified when
something was being done, such as music, reading,
chess, &c. He was fond of having a leaf of paper
and pen at hand when he was conversing, to
sketch down whatever occurred to him.

His manners were most pleasing. His features,
of the Oriental type, were handsome; a high,
thoughtful forehead, much depressed at the tem-
ples; large, expressive dark eyes, with drooping
lids, and a peculiar veiled glance through the

F

lashes; this, however, sometimes flashed distrust
or anger, sometimes happy dreaming and expec-
tancy. His nose was arched and of delicate
form, still more so the mouth, with its short
upper and full under lip, which was slightly pro-
truded and hid his teeth, when, with a slight lisp,
he pronounced the hissing consonants. An extreme mobility about his mouth betrayed every
emotion that passed within.

His bearing retained from his boyhood the
slight rocking of the head and upper part of the
body, and shifting from foot to foot; his head
was much thrown back, especially when playing;
it was always easy to see whether he was pleased
or otherwise when any new music was going on,
by his nods and shakes of the head. In society
his manners were even then felt to be distinguished. The shyness that he still retained left
him entirely during his subsequent travels, but
even now, when he wished to propitiate, he could
be most fascinating, and his attentions to young
ladies were not without effect. In his affections
filial love still held the foremost place; the veneration with which he regarded his father had in

it something religious and patriarchal; with his sisters the fondest intimacy prevailed; from his brother disparity of age still somewhat divided him. His elder sister, Fanny, stood musically most related to him; through her excellent nature, clear sense, and rich fund of sensibility (not perceptible to every one), many things were made clear to him. For his youngest sister, Rebecca, now in the bloom of her girlhood, he had an unbounded admiration, sensitive as he was to all that was fair and lovely.

Felix's nature fitted him particularly for friendship; he possessed already then a rich store of intimates, which increased as he advanced in life. To his friends he was frankly devoted, exquisitely tender; it was indeed felicity to be beloved by Felix. At the same time it must be confessed that his affection was exclusive to the utmost; he loved only in the measure as he was loved. This was the solitary dark speck in his sunny disposition. He was the spoilt child of fortune, unused to hardship or opposition; it remains a marvel that egotism did not prevail more than it did over his inborn nobleness and straightforwardness.

The atmosphere of love and appreciation in which he had been nurtured was a condition of life to him; to receive his music with coldness or aversion was to be his enemy, and he was capable of denying genuine merit in any one who did so. A blunder in manners, or an expression that displeased him, could alienate him altogether; he could then be disagreeable, indeed quite intolerable. The capital musician, Bernhard Klein, he never could bear, and simply because—as he himself confessed to me—Klein, sitting beside Felix in a box at the opera when Felix was yet a boy, whose feet when sitting on a chair did not reach the ground, impatiently muttered, "Cannot that boy keep his feet from dangling?" About such small things he could be unforgiving, for he could not use himself to hear what displeased him, and he never had been compelled to conform cheerfully to the whims of any one. I often took him to task about this, and suggested that, like the Venetian, he should keep a book of vengeance, in which to enter a debtor and creditor account for offences. I could venture to speak thus jokingly to him, for he knew that I could never have believed him capable of retaliation, even for unkindness and spite.

But his irritability, his distrustfulness even towards his most intimate friends, were sometimes quite incredible. A casual remark, a stupid jest, that he often accepted from me with perfect good temper, would sometimes suddenly cause him to drop his lids, look at me askance, and ask doubtfully, " What do you mean by that ? Now I want to know what you wish me to understand by this ?" &c., and it was difficult to restore his good humour. These peculiarities in Mendelssohn caused him, though much beloved, to be often judged unfavourably ; but those who knew him intimately accepted these few faults, the natural growth of his exceptional position, and prized none the less all that was excellent in him.

He was exquisitely kind-hearted and benevolent, even towards dumb animals. I recollect him, when a boy of thirteen, ardently pleading for the life and liberty of a small fish which had been given to his brother Paul, who wished to have it fried for himself. Felix in anger said,

"If you were anything of a boy, you would put it back in the water directly." Although the mother took the part of her nestling, the father decided the point with, "Paul, put the fish back into the water. You are no fisher, and are not entitled to his life; for pleasure or for daintiness' sake we are not to take the life of any creature." Felix joyfully seized the little fellow's hand, ran with him to the pond, and threw in the struggling fish. I have often since thought of that fish when I have seen Felix take the part of those who were in trouble.

The following note may serve as a little specimen of this:—

"DEAR EDUARD,

"A good old acquaintance of mine, the happiest fellow in the world, and the most unlucky, likewise a capital organist, intends to give a concert, when he is going to try himself in some Sebastian Bach. I have promised him to use my influence with you, to induce you, if possible, to sing for him something of Bach, perhaps 'Komm, süsses Kreuz,' or some other song or songs, in the church, with organ accompaniment. It is a question whether I have so much influence with you—but I think I have; and as the organist is an ugly fellow, who manages to get most fearfully trodden upon by reason of his being so ugly and so contented, one is bound to do the contrary, and help him along : this I would like to do, but you really can do it, if you will grant his request and give him some good advice into the bargain, for he knows very little of the world ; besides, you have studied together under Zelter, though since then you have struck out such different paths.   Addio.

"FELIX M.-B."

This considerateness guided him too in judging of others' performance ; he could not bear to find fault, and when his opinion was asked by a composer of his own works, he knew how first to commend every point that was at all commendable, and then with the greatest delicacy and firmness point out the defects. Above all he never assumed to criticise on matters of taste, every kind of pretension being foreign to his

nature.   He hated all unrealness, affectation, and
frivolity, as so much want of principle.   This
conscientiousness unmistakably ruled his musical
faculty; he was thoroughly in earnest about all
he did; the sense of duty was ever present to him,
and forbade his offering to the world anything
void of purpose, or for the mere sake of pleasing,
anything immature or frivolous, much less anything vulgar, for the artist is bound to advance
good taste and pure perception in his art.   On
this account—as even the cavillers against his
genius must admit—in the whole range of his
works there is not to be found a vulgar or trivial
thought; and for this reason, he was so very
careful in publishing.   "I have a tremendous
reverence for print," he often said to me, and
could he have foreseen his premature death, he
would have taken means to make the publication
of his immature works impossible.   On this
account, too, his fortunate social position was an
additional incentive to create according to his
highest conviction, to work unceasingly like the
very poorest, and to give only his best to the
world.

One might conclude that so moral and æsthetic a creed would imply a very grave disposition, some amount of pedantry might be suspected; but it was quite the reverse with Felix, he was of a most happy temperament. His deep convictions were never uttered in ordinary intercourse with the world; only in rare and intimate moments did they ever appear, and then only in the slightest and mostly funny allusions.* His letters bear witness to this.

The first letter he wrote to me from London, whither he had gone at the beginning of April, bears date the 19th of May, 1829.

"Dear Devrient,

"This is not intended for a letter; I have no time to write to you properly, for I have to go at four o'clock to the House of Commons, where O'Connell is to be taken to task, and afterwards to two parties (your wife will immediately

---

* Amongst many little words peculiar to him was the word "plaisir," which he mostly used for the highest kind of satisfaction.   This has been found fault with as frivolous.

say I am copying Hensel), but I consider it my
duty to take part in everything. This is but a
thanksgiving for the first letter I have received
here, which has truly gladdened me, and a prayer
to send me a few words, such as these, very often;
you will find many a blank moment, for instance
between the acts. I can picture a letter dated
'Alcidor, at the usual reading time,' or 'Agnes
von Hohenstaufen,* during Madame Milder's aria.'
In short, write me again, and soon. I have
much happiness and enjoyment here, especially
when I can shut my eyes to music and musicians,
and this fortunately is not difficult. Were I to
tell them my opinion of their music they would
think me rude, and were I to speak to them of
music generally, they would consider me quite
mad. So I do not trouble them with my notions,
but go about and look at the splendid city and
the life in its streets, or row on the river between
the bridges, merchant-vessels, and church-steeples;
or I go into the country, where spring has already
arrived with his magnificent green and blossoms
and soul-stirring perfumes; or I buy a bunch of

* Spontini's last opera.

lilies of the valley of some bawling old woman in
the crowd, and find in it somewhat more of music
than in all the concerts such as I survived yesterday, shall endure to-morrow, and put up with
again on Friday. It appears as though the impression of the 'Passion' performances were
already effaced.* I am sorry for it : the only
result of the whole affair then is to prove what
can be done, and we must content ourselves with
that result and a distant hope. That you will
not be able to attend the festival † touches me
grievously for your sake ; it would have been a
pleasure to yourself and to others. May the
devil take all rogues ! here not a few run about
unhanged, without counting the pickpockets.
Strange it seemed the other evening when I
heard the Messiah, how all the notes were the
same, how the entry of every part was precisely
in English as in German, how the music speaks
the same universal language, and yet every note

* I had sent him an account of the feeble performance of it
on Good Friday.

† I had been refused leave of absence to go to the musical
festival at Thuringia, because operas of Spontini were given
at the time.

spoke loudly that an Englishman played it, and that he did not care over-much about it. The letter was there, but the spirit was absent, and inasmuch as the letter kills, life was everywhere wanting. About the English style of singing I will say nothing, but will give you a specimen in December; you will fall from your chair with laughing; indeed, you must introduce an English singer on the stage. Neither do I like the Italian singers; the much-renowned Donizetti * is always singing sharp and roars fearfully; on the other hand, Malibran is above all praise. There are voices whose simple sound moves one to tears; she has such a one, and sings withal earnestly, passionately, and tenderly, and acts well too. You should see her! That confounded Veluti is just passing beneath the window; he is a poor wretched creature, whose singing so excited my loathing that it pursued me into my dreams that night. He sang a duet with Sontag, who is going to give a concert for the Dantzigers, where I intend (D.V.) to distinguish myself by divers flourishes. Excuse this poor letter, I have been

* Probably Donzelli.—Tr.

interrupted with visits, and my attention scattered. Farewell, remember me to your wife and children; enjoy the spring-time and be glad; we shall yet have some music together, for now art is at a standstill (in a double sense), and we shall have to make up for it. Meanwhile here is bright happy spring, and that too is good.

"Yours,

"F. M.-B."

Felix made a sensation in London. Musicians and connoisseurs were struck by such masterly powers in one so young; and in the higher circles it gave him a peculiar distinction that at their large parties, embellished by the famous artists of the season at high remuneration, he lent his aid without accepting any money, and thus belonged to the company. He was quite indignant at the way in which the paid artists were isolated from the guests, nor could he forget having seen Malibran sit in a remote corner of the drawing-room, shut out and looking miserable. The old Mendelssohn had expressed some apprehensions to me about the ardent interest Felix's

letters showed towards the great singer. I, however, was convinced that he was incapable of any
indiscretion that might divide him from his home
circle. At the same time Theresa and I were
not happy about his position in London, where
he threatened to become a drawing-room orna-
ment, and something of this may have escaped
rather bluntly in my letters, for he did not fail
to show his vexation. On the 19th of June,
1829, he wrote :—

" DEAR EDUARD,

" Your letter of the 30th May, received
yesterday, has gladdened me much, therefore I
will begin by thanking you for it. It seems
almost strange to receive news from you here, it
makes me feel how far I am away from you, and
yet it does not make me sad : indeed, when your
letter was unexpectedly handed to me at a party
last night, I had just the comfortable feeling as
if I had been asking your servant-maid whether
Herr Devrient was at home, and she, instead of
answering, went to fetch the key to open the
gate. Write often. And now I am going to

behave as if I were at Rosenstrasse, No. 1,
and going to storm a little about a passage in
your letter, for which I intend to rate you
soundly. You say that my letter has been useful
to me with your wife, who had felt so displeased
with my present mode of life, which you likewise
disapproved. If you were here I might walk up
and down your room and vent my vexation about
many things; I might, however, possibly spare you
the homily which I am going to write now, since you
cannot see my angry face. Ought anything to be
useful to me with you and your wife? Nothing
ought either to be useful or hurtful to me with
you, for I thought you knew me. At all events,
when I am once convinced that any one is sincere
with me, and that I know him, I put down the
fellow as firm and true, and life or what you will
may tug and change, in my thoughts he still
stands firm and true. What would you say to
me if I were to implore you not to be carried
away by the glitter of Spontini, but to remain
true to good music? You would charge me with
want of trust, nor would I think of making such
an appeal. But life and art are not to be

separated; and if you have no fears of my going over to Rossini or to John Bull, you must also have none that life is dragging me down. It will be some time till we meet, and if you have not full reliance on one whom you should know, you will have cause enough hereafter to feel uncomfortable about him. Now I should be sorry for this, and very sorry if anything again were to be useful or hurtful to me in your opinion, or that you thought I could ever change. Upon my word, Devrient, when I improve or deteriorate I shall let you know by express; till then believe it not (of course I mean as to certain things usually called sentiments).

" I wish many things at the devil, especially the entire last page, which is good for nothing. But I know what I mean. Now to something else. Write to me all about Agnes,* all about the theatre, what music you have in Berlin, and particularly little details of your own life; where you are going to live, with the number of the house, etc.; that does one good. You wish, my dear friend, that I should make some noise and

* " Agnes von Hohenstaufen."

éclat here: for the sake of my future prospects, I
am glad to tell you that I have already done so.
The English receive me, and are kind and pleasant
with me; for this year music is nearly over,
the season is drawing to an end; but for
conscience' sake I am going in a few days to
play Beethoven's concerto in E flat.* Musicians
think it impracticable, and say the public will eat
me; but I don't think so, and shall play it. On
the same day my 'Midsummer-Night's Dream' is
to be given, to some extent as a rehearsal for
next year, when the Philharmonic are to play it,
for I shall leave both this and the 'Calm Sea'
overture here for the winter concerts. I shall write
an opera for Covent Garden if I can be satisfied
with the librettos that they promise to show me.
They have offered me terms that are honourable,
pleasant, and advantageous; altogether the people
here like me for the sake of my music, and
respect me for it, and this delights me immensely,

---

* This refers to a concert given by Sontag for the sufferers
from an inundation on the 13th of July; but the overture was
in the interim played for the first time in public on Midsummer night at a concert, in the Argyle Rooms, of Drouet
the flute-player.—Tr.

for it is nice to have got rid of a parcel of unknown strangers and turned them into pleasant acquaintances. I get no repose nor quiet for composition, as I could in Berlin; but were I this minute to play my 'Calm Sea,' etc., to the public they would comprehend it far better than the cultivated circle in our drawing-room. Yet they understand nothing about music, which here is bad and at the worst. Then how is it? Also, by Jove, I play better here than in Berlin, and why is that? Because the people have more pleasure in listening. You will not put this down to vanity, but it is an elevating thing to feel one succeeds in giving *plaisir* to others. Answer me soon. The other night I heard Don Giovanni given by the Italians; it was funny. Pellegrini sang Leporello, and acted like an ape; at the end of his first song he introduced a string of cadences out of any half a dozen Rossinian operas; the mandoline part in 'deh vieni' was played very delicately with the bow on a violin; the second verse, however, was duly embellished, and finished somewhere up in the skies. Out of pure savageness I cried Da Capo. The commendatore had on a dressing-gown. Malibran gave a mad version of Zerlina; she made her a wild, flirting, Spanish country romp; she has an extraordinary talent. How Sontag sings Donna Anna, you know. Write soon, and love me.

"F. M.-B."

When the London season was over, Felix, in company of Klingemann, visited the Scottish lakes. Here he began, as far as rain and fog would permit, to take his first independent sketches, and under every view Klingemann added a small humorous poem. They also went to the Hebrides, and the deep impressions the lonely isles made upon Felix were recorded in the characteristic orchestral composition ("Isles of Fingal") which he finished in the following year.

Returned to London, he had the misfortune to be thrown from a cab upon the pavement, and seriously to hurt his knee. He was laid up for a long time, during which he was most carefully tended by Klingemann, whose kind offices he received with affectionate gratitude, and often tenderly alluded to them afterwards to me.

Longing for home took complete possession of him, and his bed of suffering was visited by the saddest apprehensions. He has told me that he had his cloak and travelling cap hung up within sight of his bed to comfort him, and how often he despaired of ever using them again. Much as he liked to live in London, the thought of dying there had been terrible to him.

His active restless spirit, and habit of constant work were the best aids in chasing away such dismal thoughts. His constant association with Klingemann resulted in a work which bears the impress of unclouded cheerfulness. He wrote to me about it the 29th October, 1829 :—

"I write to you this time out of generosity and wrath, for I only owe you one answer, and you promised to write to me without waiting for any answer. Now you may take it into your head also to write out of generosity, but you will not be able to do this, I hope; for with the help of God I intend to greet you myself soon after this letter arrives, and stand before you 'bowed down upon my staff.' You will find me grown thin and whiskered, and much besides, but in

certain points the same.   It is once again the old
story of internal and external.

"I have nothing to tell you, dear Eduard. I do
not like to speak of the immediate past, for it is
sad and wearisome, and to tell you about my
pleasant spring, and the singular Hebrides, I will
leave till I sit at your round tea-table, with your
wife listening—one story following another—and
after I have wished you joy on the birth of your
youngest child. I had not intended to touch
upon this subject in a letter. I could have told it
you better with a grasp of the hand, but it is too
important to be left; besides, I could not mention
the name of your wife without adding the familiar
congratulation, which means to every one just
what he likes. You must both be very happy.
Well, I shall witness it all soon, and we will have
much, very much, to chat about; for mighty projects are haunting my brain, about nice music,
old and new, that is to be performed, and in
which you may possibly be allowed to have a
part, that is to say, if you will, and if you won't
I shall thrash you. I shall suppose you will.
There are other reasons besides. It just occurs

to me that I have something to tell you after all.
I shall probably bring home with me an operetta,*
that I have written here for the silver wedding
of my parents, and that Klingemann and I
planned on our Scottish tour. It is nothing but a
little Idyll, takes place in summer-time, and in
the country, and, of course, the principal part in
it is intended for you. This is a roaming pedlar
who plays the deuce, trifles with the girls, and
filches their money; one of his pranks is to sing
a serenade, disguised as a watchman, which I
intend to write just to your voice (you know I
can do that). You will play the part splendidly,
that is to say if you will; and if you won't I shall
vide supra. Seriously, however, we will get up this
fun with other trifles, on the eve of the day, with a
regular (miniature) stage and a regular (miniature)
orchestra; and I beg of you to begin putting the
matter in hand, to think what costumes we shall
have; to take the part of stage-manager, to show
my eldest sister how she is to conduct herself as
the overseer's wife. You will know what I

* "Heimkehr aus der Fremde" (Return from abroad). The
English version is known as "Son and Stranger."—TR.

should like, and over the first rice-cake, the whole
of which I intend to eat myself, we will discuss
further particulars. Apropos! I have laughed
in my bed over Doctor Spontini; the fellow will
go mad. Altogether musical prospects in Germany are wretched. Here music is treated as a
business; it is calculated, paid for, and bargained
over, and much indeed is wanting; but the dif-
ference between a musical festival here and in Germany shows where the disparity lies. Here,
however greedy of gain and calculating they may
be, they are always gentlemen, otherwise they
would not retain their place in good society, and
this is where our court musicians fail altogther.
Devrient, when I think of the musicians of Berlin,
I overflow with gall and wormwood; they are
miserable shams, with their sentimentality and
devotion to art. I have no intention to sing the
praises of English musicians, but when they eat
an apple-pie, at all events they do not talk about
the abstract nature of a pie, and of the affinities
of its constituent crust and apple, but they heartily
eat it down. May the devil have his own!
You over in Berlin no doubt contemplate my

angry mood with all composure, and laugh at it; but another day the tables will be turned, and I shall contemplate some wrath of yours from a safe distance. So everything fits in, and we seem to me, in the midst of this weedy field of musicians, like people who, sitting in a warm, comfortable room, listen to the wind howling outside. This simile is forced upon me by the cold and wind outside, whilst I am warm beside a cosy fire. The other day, in Bala, I composed a song for you in the rain, but it is not good for much. When I now write home, towards the end I feel hurried and impatient at writing, when I would rush there myself and speak; and I will too. Till then, your F. M.-B."

During Felix's absence we had moved into a garden-house in the Mendelssohn grounds, next to the drawing-room. Hensel returned from Italy, was married to Fanny that autumn, and lived in the house on the other side of the drawing-room. Thus Felix, on his return in November, found his nearest friends installed close to him. He still was somewhat shattered, walked with a stick, and was under medical treatment for some time.

He was busy instrumenting the new operetta,
helping Fanny in the composition of a little *pièce
de circonstance*, written by Hensel, and practising
the music of these with us at the piano. They
were delightful practices, and to me every note
proclaimed the dramatic vocation of the composer.

In the distribution of the parts, besides the
domestic circle, Hensel as the overseer, Rebecca
Lisbeth, myself Kauz, we were so fortunate as to
secure the student Mantius, whose small but
charming tenor voice was much sought after in
Berlin society, for the part of Hermann. To him
the occasion was a means of furthering his private
wish to go on the stage, and he threw himself
into the task with ardour. For Hensel, entirely
devoid of musical ear, Felix had written a part
in a trio, all through upon one note, and we had
no end of trouble and fun in getting him to learn
this note. As we could not deprive the parents
too soon of their drawing-room, in which the performance was to take place, we had to rehearse
either at Hensel's or at my house, on the plain
floor, I taking upon myself the managerial cares,
and participating in all the fun and amusement

that are apt to attend amateur theatricals, and in which Felix ever was foremost. The fitting up of a stage, painting it, and making accommodation for the orchestra, had all to be accomplished on an ingeniously minute scale.

The acting rehearsals were over, lighting, costumes, all was ready and promised well, when an unexpected obstacle arose. On the very night of the *fête* I was summoned to a concert at the Crown-Prince's. These concerts usually began late, and lasted until after supper ; indeed after supper the Crown-Prince often called upon me for some German songs. This would just prevent me from taking part in the operetta, and so the *fête* would be spoiled ; and this to happen on the very eve, when everything was so well prepared, and the guests invited!

Felix was dreadfully put out at the tidings ; he was really angry. Unaccustomed to be crossed in any of his undertakings, he quite lost, in the maze of vexations he saw before him, his usual sense of what was due to the position of others. He required me to give up the court concert, which after all was no part of my regular engagement, etc.; in short, the performance of his operetta appeared to him, at that moment, the one important thing in the world. I tried to comfort him with the promise to obtain leave, if possible, to quit the concert before its termination ; and if I did not succeed in this, at all events to be back from the castle after the performance of Fanny's piece, perhaps after supper, in time for the operetta. All this, however, marred the *fête,* as it was to have been, and his excitement increased so fearfully, that when the family was assembled for the evening, he began to talk incoherently, and in English, to the great terror of them all. The stern voice of his father at last checked the wild torrent of words; they took him to bed, and a profound sleep of twelve hours restored him to his normal state.

The silver wedding-day now took its solemn course, on the 22nd of December, amid the sympathy of a large circle of friends. Anxiety as to how the evening would go off damped the children's joy somewhat, but all turned out happily. Graf von Redern kindly promised to speak for me, and took the responsibility of shortening my duties

at the concert, so that I was home by the time
Fanny's little piece was over, and quite in time for
the operetta which had been settled to come after
it. It went off with great spirit, and without a
fault, with the exception of Hensel's part in the
trio, he, as usual, not being able to catch the note,
although it was blown and whispered to him from
every side. This was, perhaps, the greatest bit of
fun of the evening for Felix; he had to bend down
over the score to conceal his laughter.

The work made a great impression on the
audience, not only by the grace of its melodies
and their tender and poetical expression, but
still more by its vein of humour, and individual-
ising of the different situations and characters;
its dramatic vitality, united to fresh musical
beauty. Every one was struck by this new
proof of Felix's special dramatic gift.

It was urged upon him to consent to a public
performance of the operetta; his mother especially
wished it, but the filial piety of Felix shrank
from exposing to the public the work which to
him was associated with a solemn occasion; there
was much in the music which had a purely

personal significance. When I praised the opening subject of the overture, he told me that it
was the bow with which he stepped before his
parents, and dedicated to them his work. Such
affectionate expressions he thought ought to
remain in the family circle. Then there was the
violoncello solo of the song No. 3, written for
his brother, the part on one note for his brother-
in-law, the compass of the part of Kauz, a
little private joke with me; all this he would not
like to be made public, perhaps to be misinterpreted. Moreover, he argued, the whole work
was not suited for the dimensions of a theatre,
for which the instrumentation would have to be
entirely remodelled. I also hinted that the slender
interest of the action would barely satisfy an exact-
ing public. Finally, I thought it would have been
most unwise to let this delicate little work follow
upon the quasi-failure of " Camacho's Wedding."

Thus it happened that the operetta was not
publicly given during Felix's lifetime; after his
death it was not to be averted. I retouched
the libretto a little, to adapt it better to stage
necessities, and if Felix no longer could remodel

the instrumentation, at all events no wants seem to have been discovered.

But from all sides he was besought, about this time, to devote himself to dramatic composition ; I, not less than others, joining in the general desire. He still believed in commissions from England, in which I had no faith at all; meanwhile he entered into relations with Holtei,* who proposed various subjects and discussed how they might be treated. He gave it up however at last, with this declaration : " Mendelssohn will never find an operatic subject that contents him ; he is much too acute." And his words have been fulfilled.

This winter brought us the most delightful intercourse. We had only to step across a yard to be with each other, and Felix made ample use of the opportunity. Now he brought a new piece of music to play us, then he wanted some verses from me, or he asked Theresa to sing

* Author of " Die Wiener in Berlin," and many other popular plays and vaudevilles; also an actor and lecturer much in vogue. In later days he turned his attention to novels; one of them, " Die Vagabunden," has had many editions.—Tr.

some songs just composed.   We painted landscape together, and he wanted me to teach him
water-colours; in return he taught me to play at
chess with all its subtleties, and laughed much
when I could never remember them.   We read
Jean Paul together a good deal, and I initiated
him in the knowledge and love of Hebel's poems.

We had much music; I was at the time
studying the part of Orestes in Gluck's "Iphi-
genia."   Felix made me study the part first in
French, in order to be quite fixed in the accents
according to the original magnificent declamation,
so often lost in an unfaithful translation.   I have
had the greatest reason to be satisfied that I
followed his advice, which also enabled me to
improve the German text.   We often sang
pieces from the operetta; he liked to hear Theresa
sing the music of Lisbeth, and when she begged
him to let her have a few of the pieces with piano
accompaniment, having already given the air of
the Evening Bells to Mantius,—one day he
brought her the pianoforte score of the entire
work in his own writing, saying that copies
should only be made with her permission.   In-

deed it was a most refined piece of courtesy. As his sisters too were often with Theresa, he found constant occasions to be with us. He played with my children, took the most minute interest in our doings, and showed all the tender and intimate sympathy that was peculiar to him.

His most serious occupation during this winter was the Reformation Symphony. He talked over the plan of it with me, and played the leading subjects in their characteristic application. With the greatest expectations I saw the work arise. In this work he tried a strange experiment in writing down the score, which I had scarcely deemed practicable. It is well known that scores are generally written by noting down only the bass, the leading phrases and effects in their appropriate lines, thus giving a complete outline of a movement, and leaving the remainder of the instrumentation to be filled in afterwards. Felix undertook to write bar by bar, down the entire score, the whole of the instrumentation. It is true that he never wrote out a composition until it was quite completed in his head, and he had played it over to those nearest to him; but nevertheless this was a gigantic effort of memory, to fit in each detail, each doubling of parts, each solo effect barwise, like an immense mosaic.   It was wonderful to watch the black column slowly advance upon the blank music paper.   Felix said it was so great an effort that he would never do it again ; he discontinued the process after the first movement of the symphony.   It had proved his power, however, mentally to elaborate a work in its minutest details.

Thus the unusually severe winter passed in delightful domestic intercourse.   We spent many evenings at the Mendelssohns' ; Hensel was at that time engaged on his large collection of portraits in pencil, and he used to draw during the evenings ; this did not check the animated flow of conversation.   The political ferment which was to explode in Paris during the July following, was much discussed.   Hensel's superloyal opinions often made Felix impatient.   Once I heard him exclaim with unusual asperity to Hensel, " You might show a little more regard for your radical brother-in-law !"   Even his father's far-seeing views of Europe's political prospects

H

at that time displeased him. "It is terrible to see one's father such a conservative!" was the only fault-finding expression I ever heard him utter of his father.

In the beginning of 1830, a musical professorship at the Berlin University (that had been created in the hope of securing him) was offered to Felix. He declined, in the conviction that such an appointment would not prove congenial to him. He suggested Marx, and through his warm advocacy obtained for his friend a social status. The elder Mendelssohn saw the continuance of this friendship with reluctance. Once he said to me, "You have such great influence with Felix, do try to free him of Marx; people of that kind, who talk so cleverly and can do nothing, act perniciously on productive minds." I believed Felix past any such dangers, especially as his approaching tour would tend to make him still more self-reliant, and said as much.*

* He became aware, in course of time, that Marx, perhaps unconsciously, aimed at separating Felix from every influence but his own. Expectations that he formed with reference to his oratorio "Moses," and the Festival of the Lower Rhine, and that Felix could not conscientiously fulfil, caused an

The spring of 1830 was approaching; the roads to Weimar, Vienna, and Italy, lay open to Felix; he was to part from home and family for some considerable time.   The date of departure was fixed towards the end of March, when on the day before, Rebecca was taken ill with the measles. She was at once separated from the rest of the family. Felix especially was denied access to her, that he might not catch the illness and be prevented from his journey.

This circumstance overwhelmed him with despair; with the grief of a lover he lamented, that without taking leave of Rebecca he could not start.   He came to us at twilight to say good-bye, anxious and cast down.   I went with him across the court, and we walked up and down a long time under the projecting eaves by the summer drawing-room, as there was a gentle rain. Felix poured himself out in almost infantine lamentations; he wept, nor was I able to comfort

---

irremediable breach between the friends. Both discovered that they had been mistaken in each other. (This may explain, though nothing can excuse the systematic depreciation with which Marx in his later writings treats Mendelssohn.—TR.)

him. "I shall never see my sister again ; who knows what may happen to her whilst I am gone? who knows what may happen to me far away? we shall never meet again!" Our conversation turned upon these words, till I almost felt super-stitious too. The next morning, before I could pay him a last promised visit, I received a note from him, one of many that had this winter flown to and fro between us. He wrote :—" The doctor gives me hope that I shall have the measles in a few days. So do not come to me, or, as Hensel says, Noli me tangere."

Now his journey was put off, and as soon as he could leave his bed he had the pleasure of spending the period of convalescence with Rebecca. As both were forbidden to exert their eyes, ingenuity was set to work to keep off *ennui*, which led to many merry pranks. Our inter-change of despatches across the court was carried on by Felix through Fanny's hand, to whom he dictated his droll missives. One example :—

" Thousand thanks for your letter, send more soon, to-morrow I reply at length. Whilst we are here eyeless and deedless, could you not send me

that game with blocks, or the puzzle of pictures, to
be put together, that I gave your children some
years ago at the ' Kälbermarkt ?' it would now
be a nice serious occupation for me. In case
it is lost, send it me by bearer, or quod Deus
vult.

" FIREMAN, DRIVER, & Co."

Another frolicsome dictation. " Amongst my
daily correspondents in England, Hungary,
South America, and Provence, why should I not
count thee, O royal singer?   Though thou be
disguised in a thousand forms, yet, charmer, I
know it is thou (from Goethe's Divan, on which
you now are probably sleeping) ; that is to say,
I rejoice heartily at your success as Barber, Arch-
angel, and Saviour. Few people can boast of
such progressiveness, and it has caused a Berlin
eye to look askance at you to-day in the paper.
I have no news to tell you, as my invention is at
a standstill. But what is all that about spring
in your letters ? Does spring consist of water-skins
for the heavens and umbrellas for the earth, and
are good fires and chattering teeth essential to it ?
I do not believe in spring at all. In my con-

dition, what are love, or art, or spring? Love grows not bitter, my stomach however does; love ever flies back, so does my stomach-ache. I shall do like a revered personage, and hold by the practical,* which however in my present case is miserable.

"Till here this letter is to be burnt, or torn up; what follows may remain alive, viz., how glorious is this wide world of God! Write to me soon again. I have been practising Cramer's first study with hands crossed; I play the institution of the Supper from the Passion upon a dumb-flute. I loiter about idle, like any Kapellmeister. You ask when will come my Easter? Sunday, my dear fellow, or Monday; but if you think to start before me, you are strongly mistaken. We shall probably exit at different sides together. I have nothing rational to say, so will finish till to-morrow,

"Yours,

(*autograph*) "FELIX MENDELSSOHN-BARTHOLDY."

Sister and brother were at last restored to

---

* I had met with this expression in Dinter's new version of the Bible; its singularity had struck us, and we often made use of it.

health. It was May, and Felix, full of life and spirits, cured of his over-irritability, was considered fit for his journey. Our intercourse during the winter had bound us very close together; we both were loth to part, but Felix's loving nature felt it the most. When I had said my farewells, and accompanied him down the doorsteps, I was parting from him with a shake of the hand (I was always averse to the embracing of men). He called me back after the first steps, and with the most tender and appealing expression, said, " I think you might have put your arms round me." With all my heart I did it, and thus parted from the charming youth.

How Felix enjoyed and utilised his most delightful tour is well known to the readers of his first series of letters; my relations with him at this time the following letters will show. The first he wrote from Vienna and Styria :—

" Vienna, September 5th, 1830.

" MY DEAR EDUARD,

" I do not see why I should not write to you, as it is particularly cosy and twilighty here

just now, whilst outside it is storming and rain-
ing.   I have just finished composing, and am
naturally thinking of you, who are to hold forth
in it.   Therefore I will write to you, although you
are not generous, or you would not have waited
until I had answered your welcome letter, but
would have written and told, and told and sketched
me a thousand little things, as you know so well
how to do when you like.   Well, as long as you
give a satisfactory account of yourself now I will
be satisfied, but write me soon a long letter, four
sheets, with gossip, pictures, and notes ; in fact,
chat with me.   I should think you sometimes
longed to do so ; it is not a thing one longs for
singly, and I do so very often.   Let me know
what and how you are singing, how your white
morning jacket is, and whether you are painting.
Tell me about your wife, and whether she often cries
over some stupid critique about you in the paper,
and you have to go to the office (this time without me) to set the matter right.   Then long for
me and write to me directly.   I must also know
whether your sister-in-law still respects my
Reformation Symphony, and that you are all as

pleasant together as ever. Tell me whether Felix still has his hopeful spirits, and is the same capital naughty boy; whether Marie is still my friend (I maintain that she has a weakness for me ever since that affair in the garden, you remember I did not bow to her); finally, watch and listen whether Anna, and especially your wife, have forgotten my upsetting the children's chaise; and do you think of me when you have a rice cake? In a word, say good-day to me. Am I strange because I am far away?

"I am certainly far away, and it is a long while since we saw each other. When I sing anything out of the 'Heimkehr' now, it sounds sadly like a remembrance of the past. I have had a merry life since then, and felt happy, but have made little music. If Vienna were not so confoundedly dissipated, so that I have to creep into myself and write something sacred, I should have made nothing new. To-day I have finished the second movement of a Choral with instruments, and expect to finish the third the day after to-morrow, and so on till the whole is completed. After that I intend to put down a little Ave Maria for voices

alone, that I have already finished in my head.
In the Choral, that you will receive as soon as
it is done, you will find an aria for your voice;
have the goodness to sing it in a state of anguish.
Hauser* swears, because my bass parts and songs
are written so high; this gives me occasion to say
that they suit you; and what though I needs
must sing my own youthful songs miserably
myself, the epilogue that follows turns out a
flattering allusion to you.

" *Lilienfeld Convent, October 2nd.* At this point
I was interrupted four weeks ago; left the letter
unfinished, and have had no quiet since. I send
you this from Styria. The convent is quite
enclosed by green wooded hills; there is a rushing
and murmuring on every side; the consequence
is trout for supper. It is now only seven o'clock,
and already quite dark; this reminds one of
autumn, no less than by day do the thousand
tinted hills, where the red of the cherry trees and
the pale-green of the winter corn gleam gaily
through each other. I went in the twilight to

* Baritone, then at the Kärnthnerthor theatre, afterwards
director of the conservatorium at Munich.

the convent and made acquaintance with the organ. To-morrow I am off southward, and a big parcel of time again lies behind me. Meanwhile I have received your very dear letter with the view of the garden, for which I heartily thank you; my regrets on the last page might have been spared, but as they are there let them stand for the next occasion, or when I am in Rome; they will still apply. My Choral is finished long ago, and the Ave also; I will send them you by the first safe opportunity; a song has also been born since then, but as it is good for nothing I shall keep it for myself. Moreover, I have been, alas! making love in Baden, and felt the pains and pleasures; it was hard to part, for it was nice; I may never find it so nice again, but it could come to nothing. This morning, being sure of that, I took my leave. Also, yesterday, I was walking in the morning with a party of ladies, in elegant morning dress (you know it, from *Fra Diavolo**), dined luxuriously, and in the evening improvised on themes of songs; to-day, however, I am as rusty as ever.

* I had played the "lord" in this opera.

The road went through the autumnal hills, the
air was cold ; I long to be off again, and here the
aforesaid trout make their appearance. It is
wretchedly dull here in Lilienfeld ; one hears the
cracking of whips from the high road—a great
way off. Now, after dinner, things look more
pleasant, and I will tell you a few more ' since
thens.' So I have been to Presburg to see the
coronation ; I have written the particulars to
Paul. It was vexatious, as I was walking beside
the cathedral, amongst the handsome Hungarians,
with their fine faces, their lithe and gallant forms
and brilliant costumes, to meet a well-known
Berlin acquaintance. The Mark * is truly a
sandy region ; the sight of my beloved country-
man made me feel low-spirited. You know that
when I begin to abuse I go on at it for some
time, and so I will take this opportunity to tell
you that I was little pleased with the painters at
Munich. They are wanting in the first quality
that I think an artist ought to have, and that is
reverence. They speak about Peter Paul Rubens
as if he was one of them, or indeed scarcely so

* Berlin lies in the " Mittelmark," a very sandy tract.—TR.

high; and think they glorify Cornelius when they arrogantly disparage another great artist, whose worst picture they will never understand. I wish the devil would take the odious vanity that is the order of the day now! By heaven! these people do not know anything beyond their tiresome 'I,' and that is the reason they are so faint-hearted. There is Czerny, for instance, he thinks of nothing in the world but of himself, his credit, his fame, his money, his popularity. What is the consequence? He is thought little of in Vienna, no longer considered even as a pianist; and although he has constantly, even whilst giving his lessons, music-paper and pen and ink at his side, to give forth his ideas when he cannot retain them any longer, even the publishers shrug their shoulders and think "the public is no longer so responsive as it used to be." At the Kärnthnerthor one wretched thing after the other is given; a respectable opera has not been heard for years, only Auber, and at most "Guillaume Tell." No one goes to the opera, and those who do go are bored, and yet the people do not take a lesson. Until some fire falls from heaven

things will not mend. (Tranquillo.) To proceed.
I have been staying a few days at Hauser's, who
has been exceedingly kind and cordial to me.
Amongst other things, he has given me a tiny
book of Luther's Songs, to take with me on my
travels, that will give me much to compose.
Apropos, please to ask Marx whether he has sold
my 'Tu es Petrus,' to Simrock of Bonn, and
let me know whether or not, *stanto pede* in
German. (You will be allowed also to add some
other news.) They have offered me in Vienna to
engrave the score, so if nothing comes of it in
Bonn, I will accept, and dedicate it to the Pope
or to the Duchess of Dessau, or some one else.
I say, Devrient, I am sleepy, and as we shall
have no more music together this day, I will go
to bed. Think of me sometimes, write often,
and remember me to your wife and sister-in-law
most affectionately.

"Let me also ask you to excuse me to Baur, for
not having answered him yet. I have become
so lazy with my pen, and write so badly, that I
may be forgiven. But you know what I mean;
when the head is giddy with thinking of the

Styrian hills, Venice, the Assumption of the Virgin by Titian, etc., writing and many other things are forgotten. The main things, however, are not—and so good-night.

"F. M.-B."

When Felix, after the suggestive experiences described in his letters from Rome and Naples, was returning to Germany, through Florence, Genoa, and Milan, he wrote to me from the last-named town, under date the 13th July, 1831.

"DEAR DEVRIENT,

"You will be angry with me for my long silence, but it has happened unfortunately with me. Six months ago I wrote you a short but explicit letter, and put into it a new song for you, and a few words that cannot be repeated, as what has been warmly felt would only come out cold and dry if told a second time. As I was truly anxious you should receive this letter, since it could not be copied, I put it myself in the post; nevertheless, you have not had it. This has

annoyed me; whenever I felt inclined to write
to you, I felt as if I ought to repeat that letter
and send you something with music; then I
thought it might again be lost, and so felt con-
strained, and put off writing altogether. But it
is going on too long now that we hear nothing
from each other; I know not even where you
are; it may be in Paris, Berlin, or Pekin. As I
am preparing to leave Italy, it occurs to me that
you have not received a single letter of mine
from this country. This must not be, and therefore I will hastily scribble a few lines before going
over the Simplon. I still owe you a reply to
your last letter, which put me quite out of
humour for a while, and I was on the point of
thinking that in essential things we did not quite
understand each other; when at the right moment
it happily struck men not to rely on any letter, but
only on the fact that after all we do understand each
other. And the last thought was right, for the
mood of the hour, on which the tone of the letter
much depends, changes; but the essentials, such
as our relations towards each other, do not. Is
it not so? You reproach me that I am twenty-

two and not yet famous.* To this I can answer nothing ; but if it had been the will of God that at twenty-two I should be famous, then famous I most likely should be. I cannot help it, for I compose as little with a view to becoming famous as of becoming a Kapellmeister. It would be delightful to be both, but as long as I am not positively starving, I look upon it as my duty to compose just how and what my heart indites, and to leave the effect it will make to Him who takes heed of greater and better things. As time goes on I think more deeply and sincerely of that,—to write only as I feel, to have less regard than ever to outward results, and when I have produced a piece that has flowed from my heart—whether it is afterwards to bring me fame, honours, orders, or snuff-boxes, does not concern me. We were quite agreed upon this, and it was the principal subject of a conversation we had in my little

* I had in jest quoted the line in Schiller's "Don Carlos," " Two and twenty years, and nothing done for immortality." I had added that by writing Psalms and Chorals, even if they recalled Seb. Bach, one would not become famous, and had referred him again to the composition of operas. This had nettled him.

room opening on the court, in consequence of which conversation we called each other 'Du,' struck up an acquaintance, and passed some tolerably pleasant evenings together. But if you think that in my development, or in my productions, or in myself, there is anything neglected or overlooked, then tell me clearly and exactly what that is, and in what it consists. It would certainly be a severe reproach. You want me to devote myself to operas, and think it is wrong in me not to have done so long ago. I respond: give me a really good text, and in a few months it shall be composed; every day I long anew to write an opera. I know I could produce something bright and fresh, but I have no words. And a libretto that does not quite kindle my enthusiasm I am determined not to set. If you know any man capable of writing an opera, tell me his name for heaven's sake, I am only looking for him. But until I have a libretto would you prefer me to do nothing (even supposing I could)? That I have lately written only sacred things was a necessity to me, just as one feels sometimes an irresistible impulse to read one

certain book—it may be the Bible—and finds
happiness only in reading it. If my music is
like Seb. Bach, it is again no fault of mine, for
I wrote it as I felt at the time ; and if the words
have suggested the same musical thoughts to me
that they did to old Bach, I shall value them
all the more. For I know you do not mean
that I copy his form without his purport ; if it
could be so, its emptiness would disgust me too
much to write it down. I have been writing
a large composition that perhaps will one day
make some effect, ' The first Walpurgis night '
of Goethe. I began it simply because it pleased
me and excited me ; I did not think of any
performance. But now that it is finished, I see
that it is well suited for a large concert piece,
and in my first subscription concert in Berlin
you shall sing the bearded Druid—the chorus
sung by —, kindly assisted by —. I have written the part of the Druid into your throstle (by
permission), and you will have to sing it out
again. As I have always found that those pieces
which I have written with the least regard for
people have pleased them best, so I suppose it

will be with this one.　I only say this that you
may see how I still hold to the *practical*, though
generally when it is too late; but who the d——
can write music, which is the most unpractical
thing in the world (that is why I love it so
much), and think of what is practical!　It would
be much as if some one were to set his declaration
of love into rhyme and metre, and write it to his
lady-love.　I am now going to Munich, where
they offered me a libretto, to see if anything in
the shape of a poet is to be found there.　A man
who has a little luck and wit I want; he need
not be a giant.　If I cannot find one there I will
perhaps make Immermann's acquaintance on this
particular account; and if he too is not the man I
seek, I will try London, and once more beat up
Klingemann.　It always appears to me that the
right fellow has not appeared yet, and what shall
I do to find him out?　He does not live at
Hotel Reichmann, nor next door; write to me
about this.　Although it is my belief that Pro-
vidence sends all, including opera librettos, when
they are wanted, we too must not be behindhand,
but spy and search—and I wish the libretto

were there! Meanwhile I am composing as good things as ever I can, and that I am not responsible for the result we have settled long ago in my little room; the official documents were there drawn out, and cannot be altered. But enough now of dry matters; I have almost become cross and impatient again, although it is against my resolve. It is pleasant living here. This is a city of plane trees, all embowered in avenues of them, gardens, with fields of rice and maize, and round the walls inside and outside there runs a double avenue of plane trees. Here one drives in the afternoon, and has a peep at the rank and fashion.

"But if you suppose that there are any Italian singers in Italy, you are profoundly in error. The prima donna in Rome is a native of Berlin. O misery! she sang execrably, and gave herself as many airs as a horse with bells; she likewise failed. The best songstress at present in Italy is said to be a lady called Unger (Tedescha). The first bass is Herr Schoberlechner, from Vienna; he calls himself Schober here — the *lechner* is not to be expected from the Italians.

All the good singers I have heard in Paris and London, where they are all assembled now, and draw the mediocre ones after them, so that only those lamentably deficient remain at home. Thus it is not to be wondered at that I would rather hear Italian music in Paris, where, in the first place, all the first singers are; in the second place, all the second best; thirdly and fourthly, where there are chorus and orchestra. You can have no conception of an Italian chorus. As I was supposed to be in the land of music, I thought I would try and recognize one good voice amongst the chorus; but they were all vile, roar like quacks at a fair, and are always (without exception) a crotchet before or behind the orchestra. Then the orchestra is composed of wind instruments out of tune and screaming fiddles, and does not go together. I swear to you that the opera at Wittenberg (whether there is one there or not) is better than the San Carlo at Naples. No German can have an idea of what it is here —that is to say, no real German; for such a one as I lately met here is as much a real German as cheese and beer. Fancy, Devrient, the fellow's

expenses are *paid for two years* by the ministry,
in order that he may study Italian music, and
on his return teach the Italian method of singing, and introduce, as he unblushingly told me,
the new operas of Donizetti and Bellini. Alas!
you have no idea of the extent of these horrors.
Could you but hear one of these Italian-taught
singers, what a total absence of all method they
have; how much better and more purely a Bavarian barmaid sings than they ; how they ape
the little originalities, naughtinesses, and exaggerations of the great singers, and call *that* method.
This is what is to be introduced amongst us, who
have so much better things. There is in all Italy
no singer like Schätzel, and you know I am by
no means one of her most ardent admirers. The
great fault with them all is the seeking to Italian-
ize themselves, whilst what our northern nature
has given them is the best and only good they
have. Do you imagine that there are voices in
Italy like Milder's, Schechner's, Sontag's ; that
there is a Haitzinger, a Bader, a Mantius, or a
Wild (I omit all mention of basses, not to wound
your modesty) ? Nevertheless it is true. O ye

ungrateful! I will say no more, for I preach to
deaf ears. I only wish I could hear a song from
you, or a few fresh high notes from your wife
again, irrespective of all friendly considerations.
Where here are there such bright glad voices?
One has but to listen to the common people singing with their nasal twang. And yet it is a land
of art, because it is a chosen land of nature,
where there is life and beauty everywhere; in
the blue sky, in the sea, and the trees, there is
music enough. But the land of the artist is
Germany; long may it live! The other day I
met the engraver Schmidt, whom I once saw at
a party at your house; his wife had brought some
songs of Taubert with her, and as you had spoken
about these songs, I asked her to lend them to me.
They have given me a great and genuine pleasure,
for there is character and soul in every one,
and some phrase, some trait, which clearly tells
that it is the thought of a true musician. I
was also pleased on my own account, for I had
begun to fear that I was becoming quite churlish,
and had no longer any joy in what is new (as can
be seen on the preceding page); but not at all,

for when the right thing appears I am truly overjoyed, and may God grant that Taubert is or is likely to be such a man as peeps out of his songs. But he must write other things besides songs, and of these not such sweet ones, but fiery ones, rough, uncouth, wild ones; he must burn and rave a little, I think, until he comes to himself. Give the man thanks and greeting from me, and tell him I had thoughts of writing to him about his songs, to shout a *bravo* to him across the Alps, and make a few marginal notes. Afterwards it occurred to me, however, that there are such very polite people in Berlin, who cannot bear anything of the kind, and would take umbrage—in short, I left it alone. Most likely you will scold me for this, but in any case write me something about him, where he stands, and whether he will and must advance. The end of the ' Brook '— 'Say, brooklet, does she love me?' where the brook keeps on nodding and saying, ' O yes'— is delicious. And now it is the 19th, and in an hour I enter the carriage on the one side, the Schmidts on the other, and we drive to the Lake of Como. There we bathe this evening; fly about to-morrow in a steam-boat; climb over mountains to Lugano the day after, and I have just bought Keller's map of Switzerland, with its blue snow mountains. How I ever and everywhere think fondly of you all I need not say. Continue to love me, and remember me cordially to your sister-in-law, your wife, and children. It will not be so bad to be amongst you once again. But let me know how all are, and what you are doing, and herewith I say farewell to you all from Italy. I am now bound northward again. Till then,

"FELIX M.-B."

Once more he wrote to me from Switzerland, after having traversed its western portion, from Lucerne, the 27th August, 1831.

"YOU VERY DEAR FAMILY,

"Thanks for your letter from the bottom of my heart; it is a real good family letter, and made me feel as though I had just been spending the evening with you. I cannot leave off reading it over and over again, because out of every word beams the joyful happiness you have in common, and your full consciousness of it, in which I am remembered. If I could only tell you how refreshing is such a letter, then there would be no need to thank you. It is nice of you to be so happy whilst the world is raving, and to be quietly progressing, only closing your shutters against the storm and hail outside. All besides is evil. To you, dear Mrs. Devrient, I must send a special acknowledgment for your kind lines and remembrance. You cannot think how kind it was of you to write me a greeting yourself, and in the very words in which you would have spoken it. As I said above, I have been spending an evening with you, which has always been a pleasant, happy time.

" You tell me to make haste and return ; and you, Eduard, say that my mother is inclined to extend my stay from home. I fancy none of us quite know how it will be—it is difficult to adhere to any strict plan in travelling. I should like to get a good deal of first-rate work done before I return to Berlin. As I stand at present I shall hardly find employment there; a few

concerts are not of much account, and more
than that I do not expect to achieve in Berlin.
Therefore I want to devote myself again as soon
as possible to composition. During my whole
Italian journey (which has undoubtedly advanced
me much) I have, in the opinion of people, made
no progress, and consequently must have gone
back. I therefore want soon to show myself in
something tangible. This time of war and epi-
demic is not the most favourable, but yet it must
be, and I have no fear. The thing in which all
my wishes would meet would be an opera; for I
confess to you for the last six months I have had
an incredible longing to set about one. I cannot
think of instrumental music now, because I have
nothing but voices and choruses buzzing around
me, and I shall have no peace till I have worked it
out. Alas! I feel that the opera I should write
now would not be nearly as good as a second one
that I might write hereafter; and that I must
enter upon the new path that is in my thoughts,
and make some way upon it before I can be sure
whither it will lead me—and how soon. I
already begin to feel sure, in instrumental music,

what I ought to strive after, and because I have accomplished more in it, work with more certainty and clearness. In short, the spirit moves me. To this is added that during these last days I have become horribly humble-minded, quite through chance, which chance, however, has set me thinking.   In the Engelberg valley I found ' Wilhelm Tell ' of Schiller, and as I read it again I felt the old rapture and happiness at such a divine masterpiece, and at the fire and enthusiasm that breathes in it.   All at once there occurred to me a word of Goethe, who, in the course of a long conversation about Schiller, once said to me, ' Schiller was able to supply two five act tragedies every year, besides other poems.'   This trade expression, ' supply,' struck me forcibly, and as I read the fresh glowing poem, a sense of the prodigious industry out of which it had sprung came over me, and it seemed to me as if in my life I had as yet accomplished nothing of any mark.   All I have done appears to me somewhat miscellaneous ; I feel as if I too would like to ' supply ' something.   Think me not arrogant, pray, but be sure I only say this because I know what *ought* to be, and is not.

But where I shall find such an opportunity, how
I am to set about finding it, I have till this day
not been able to fathom. If there is such a task
for me, I shall find the opportunity—that I firmly
believe; and if I do not find it, I shall know it
was reserved for another. But then wherefore
would have been this great longing? In short,
I must compose; that is the sum of my long
speech.* Thus you see we are radically of one
mind, though I like to use my privilege of retort-
ing to all your little growls. And so permit me
to growl a little longer about what you write to
me of being at work on the libretto of a comic
opera for Taubert, without adding a word about
the subject, the plot, etc. Why do you not let
me know what it is that you are working and
thinking at? What name has it? what is the
list of characters? and will there be drums and
trumpets in the orchestra? I am uncommonly
glad that Marschner is composing 'Heiling,'
especially as I believe that no one living could
compose it so well, and that the opera will make
a great effect. The fault you justly charge him

* " Der langen Rede kurzer Sinn " (Wilhelm Tell).—TR.

with, of dependence on Weber, is one to which
your poem in its very nature tends; but if this
circumstance should rouse him to avoid the temp-
tation of being quite so Weberish as heretofore,
the opera will have a more natural flow, and become his best.   Moreover his ' Templar' is so
great an advance upon its predecessors, that no
doubt 'Heiling' will still improve upon the
' Templar,' and you may expect much joy from the
work.   What gives me the most pleasure is your
saying that you have outgrown the phase from
which ' Heiling' was produced, and that your
libretto for Taubert will show it.   I shall watch it
with the greatest interest, for what you say of
your aspirations in this direction I fully concur in,
making due allowance for sundry expressions of
self-disparagement, as, for example, when you say
you feel yourself wanting in a wider range of
study.   The only thing that seemed to me
wanting in the one libretto of yours that I know,
was a certain spontaneity in the incidents and
characters; it appeared to me as though you
still thought too much of the theatre.   If you can
attain to placing upon the stage men and natural

actions, instead of actors and scenic effects, then I am certain you will produce the best opera texts that we are likely to have ; for to be versed in dramatic affairs as you are is to be unable to produce anything undramatic. And besides I cannot think what you would have altered in your verses. If they have sprung from within, and have been felt with reference to truth and to music, then they will be beautiful and musical, although they may not read flowingly in the libretto. For the matter of that, write prose ; we will find a way to set it to music—where there is an inward need the outward expression is soon found ; but to transfer mere form into form, when verse is musically manufactured and not musically thought, when pretty words are spun out to hide the void of true life within, this, I agree with you, is a fix out of which there is no escape.

" Heavens ! here am I inditing a homily, for which I am little fitted ; excuse it, and do as you require me to do, take the purport of what I say, and never mind the inappropriate illustration. The mouth will overflow with that which fills the heart, and so surely as that neither pure metre, good thoughts, beautiful language, will ever constitute a good poem, without a certain flash of poetry that streams through the whole, so surely an opera can only be perfectly musical (and consequently perfectly dramatic) when there is a true sense of natural life in all its characters. There is a passage of Beaumarchais about this, who was accused of not letting his characters express fine thoughts and poetical feelings often enough. He replied that it was not his fault. He owned that whilst he wrote he was in incessant and animated conversation with his characters across the writing-table; that he would call out: 'Figaro prends garde, le Comte sait tout—Ah! Comtesse, quelle imprudence!—Vite, sauve toi, petit page;' and whatever they answered him he wrote down, nothing else. This appears to me very nice and true. But I am talking like a book; away with it. You must answer me about this, so that we may growl at each other again; it is not unprofitable to interchange one's ideas about many things from a distance, it leaves time to eat one's rice afterwards, though I had done better to begin my letter with this. In

K

the evening, when I turn in, cross and wet through
with the storm, at a clean, smooth, brown Swiss
farmhouse (the walls consist entirely of windows,
the furniture of thick-built stoves, high beds, and
flowerpots), and have looked through every
window, to enjoy the sight of just such other
houses, and the mountains towering behind them,
I order a ' Swiss rice,' which is then my great
restorative. Alas! I have to eat it all alone (the
alas applies to ' alone,' not to ' eat it all'). Had
I begun with telling you this I should not have
quitted the subject of Switzerland, for there is no
land like it. No dreams or pictures can give any
idea of what it contains in beauty. Besides, it
is so unique, so entirely different from other
lands in everything, from the shapes of the
mountains to that of the houses, that it must be
seen to be known. Every mountain has its
peculiar character and physiognomy, be it frown-
ing or smiling, old or youthful. One stands here
facing the entire scale of nature ; one takes in all
the seasons at a glance, from the valley lying in
the summer sun, to the naked rock ; and above
again, to the region of snow and ice, with all the

mists and storms of winter; and then again from
the fields of ice one looks deep down into the
green valley blooming with trees and herbs.   Is
there no possibility for you once to see Switzerland?   For it gives one a new conception of the
bountiful God, and His nature with its infinite
loveliness.   Every man who can, should once in
his life see Switzerland.   What is parched Italy
in comparison with this fresh life and sound
healthfulness?   One cannot possibly know what
' verdure '   means,   what   meadows,   waters,
springs and rocks can be, unless one has been
here.   But what is the use of writing?   Never
have I felt so free, so on a par with nature as I
have during these never-to-be-forgotten weeks;
and I am determined, if ever I can again roam
about for a few weeks during the summer, it
shall be amongst these mountains.   But I have
composed nothing new since, excepting a few
songs.   I wish I could really spend an evening
with you and play you my ' Walpurgis Night,'
or what is better, you could sing it to me ; it lies
well for you.   Your plot for a libretto with
the Italian Carnival and the act in Switzerland I

knew already, but did not know it was yours; you can guess who told me of it. Have the goodness to make Switzerland immensely and above all measure hearty. If you picture a tender Switzerland, with Jodeln and 'Sehnsucht,' as I had to witness yesterday at the theatre in the 'Swiss family,' with sentimental hills and Alphorns, I shall make an effort and write a crushing critique about you in the Spenersche Zeitung. But no! please to make it jolly, and let me hear more about it. Above all, send me the promised music of Taubert, and, if possible, something from your opera. I shall write to him to-day and acknowledge his little note. Keep your promise about the letter to Munich, you dear ones, and fail not to refresh me again with it. And now I must go, for it is a fine day, and to-morrow I shall probably ascend the Righi; so to all farewell, and remain well. My kindest regards to your sister-in-law. I wish her joy of her convalescence, which I hope will continue. The country people here say, 'Grüss eu Gott!' So be it, and good-bye. Continue to love me.

"FELIX M.-B."

How he travelled eastward in Switzerland, and went over the lake of Constance to Munich, is known from his published letters. Also, how he received the text for an opera, went to Düsseldorf to consult with Immermann about it; how he informed his father of this, from Paris (in December), and how he contended against his father's proposition to seek a French libretto. I had already disputed this plan with the elder Mendelssohn; Felix's written objections exhaust the subject. I have two communications to add to the printed letters from Paris before the visit to London in April, 1832.

"Paris, January 5th, 1832.

" DEAR FRIEND,

" So guilty as I am towards you I never yet was to friend. Will you still deign to know me? Or do you turn away from me since I have forgotten the way to write? I have no excuse to offer; the only possible one would be that I had not received your letter; but I dare not falsify; I have undoubtedly received it, in Munich, and your libretto * gave me the greatest

* " Die Kirmes." Opera in one act, written for Taubert.

pleasure. I have read it many times, and rejoice in the unmistakable progress that it shows. That this progress gives me more pleasure than it can to any one else, you know, and I need not say it; but how much better this libretto appears to me than your former ones, how much more heartfelt and true it is, that I must needs tell you now. Our correspondence and confabulations show that we are of one opinion, and that from you we may expect the best of librettos seems quite clear to me. We shall soon meet and talk it over, and then you must recollect your old promise to write something for my stomach, in return for which I shall compose for yours, then we shall each devour something for our own. I shall sing vilely, you a little better; in return, you play a little worse, and I still cannot paint; in a word, then we shall return to all our old ways. We are still as we were, and you are not angry with me; is it not so? Upon this you are to write two lines instantly, and tell me if you will have anything more to do with me, so that I may take a long breath and go in for a good gossip; there is no mistake about my being in the wrong towards

you. I felt this so much when I got your letter
(forwarded from Rome), and read the date,
'May,' upon it, in which you express so much
friendly anxiety about me, and had been praising
my compositions to Count Redern; in which you
speak of the garden, of heat, fruit, and cholera,
which are all over now, in the height of the
giddy season of fashion, in December. It made
me feel strange, and I thought, ' He is not the
one to be offended with you, because you are as
you are,' and so I took heart and wrote. But
when you answer this I shall reply somewhat
more in detail, for I have much, very much,
to tell you, and there is much for us to discuss
before I return to Berlin, so that when I am there
we shall have discussed and have only to act.
And now be still my friend, and farewell.
May it be with you, your wife, and the children,
as I would wish. And that is settled ? we
understand each other.

" FELIX M.-B.

"P.S.—I have not replied to Marie and Felix;
I must beg you to deliver the enclosed, which
will be my justification."

"Paris, 10th March, 1832.

" DEAR EDUARD,

"Writing is to me just now what speaking is to a dumb man ; but I must from time to time give you and yours a sign of life, so that you may not quite forget that such a person as I is in the world, and also that I may receive a sign of life in return from you. You are of such arithmetical exactness, properly speaking you never write, but only answer. At all events do so now, although I am not going to ask anything. I am only going to say that I look forward with particular enjoyment to being again with you and yours. Please God I shall soon make my appearance, and then look to it how you will get rid of me again. I promise Marie and Felix a great deal of fun and nonsense ; we must have some more games at horses. I promise you a quantity of new music, and if you will promise me some rice-cake and preserves, and some singing, the preliminaries may be considered settled. Shall we paint again ? A few days ago Madame Beer told me quite pleasantly that you were fearfully ill, Madame Schneider had told

her so. I rush off, find Madame Schneider has
gone to a party. I follow her to a strange house,
make my bow to the ladies and gentlemen, say,
'*permettez,*' the ladies regarding my shabby
coat with silent admiration. Madame Schneider
appears scarcely to know me. I ask her to be
good enough to tell me about this news. She refers me to her daughter, who sits at the piano, and
at last brings out, her brother had written to her
two months ago that you had had a cough. Here-
upon I made a joyful exit, and resolved to write to
you directly, to thank you for being so kind
as to inhabit the earth. I have become nervous
here in Paris, for I have received bad news.*
But now I look forward to our meeting, and
I rejoice that Madame Beer, Madame Schneider,
her daughter, and her daughter's letter were in
the wrong; this is the meaning of my letter.

*　　*　　*　　*　　*

"I have something to ask of you, Eduard, which
you must answer me directly. I am to compose
an oratorio for the Cecilia Society, and as I
shall not be able to commence my opera in any

* Of the death of his friend Eduard Rietz.

case before July, and most likely not till after
that, I shall have between next month and then
a glorious quarter of a year, in which I could
complete at least a portion of the oratorio, for
which I have already many designs in my head.
The subject is to be the Apostle Paul; the first
part the stoning of Stephen and the persecution;
the second part the conversion; the third, the
Christian life and preaching, and either his
martyrdom or taking leave of his congregation.
I should like the words to be chiefly from the
Bible and hymn-book, and a few free passages
(the little Christian flock would sing perhaps the
chorals in the first part,—I would take the
defence of Stephen from the Bible). But I cannot put these texts together myself. Will you
do it? You are better acquainted with the Bible
than I, and know exactly what I want; it would
give you little trouble. You could do it; tell me
if you will; then we will write further on the
subject, for no more time must now be lost.
Good-bye; regards to your wife, your sister-in-
law, your children, your entire household, and be
well and happy.   " FELIX M.-B."

I did not feel equal to this trust; my standard of the importance of the framework of an oratorio was too high for me to think my Bible authority sufficiently secure. I therefore counselled him to apply to our theological friends, Baur and Schubring, who would undoubtedly furnish him with ample materials for the work. He did so, and continued corresponding with them for years, not only for "St. Paul," but also for the construction of "Elijah."

In July, 1832, Felix returned to Berlin. He found us removed to another house, also in a garden,—we had given up that in the Mendelssohn grounds to Hensel, who had it fitted up as a studio for himself and his pupils.

The two years during which we had been separated had in no wise estranged us; our intercourse was resumed upon the old footing. Felix was the same warm-hearted, merry friend. The children were familiar as ever; he made the old unforgotten jokes, insisted on their calling him "Mr. Councillor," they likewise insisting on calling him "Mr. Horrid." He invited himself as of old

to the favourite rice-cake, and when he happened
to call at our dinner-time (that repast being at a
later hour at his father's), he would seat himself
at a corner of the table and ask for a little of this
or that dish.   He could eat at almost any time,
as well as sleep, and confirmed the saying of
Jean Paul, "All good people eat much," by bright
example.

In sad moments also he opened his heart to us,
so far as this lay in his nature.   Thus he told us,
the first evening he spent with us, that he had
been that day to the house of his friend Eduard
Rietz, and followed the traces of his last moments.
We spoke of the excellent qualities of the
deceased, when Felix suddenly broke off, took a
turn through the room, and stopped before the
piano, saying he wanted to hear the well-known
sound once again.   He preludised, spoke of the
touch and tone of the instrument, and gradually
got absorbed in an improvisation that lasted
above an hour.   We sat motionless, devoutly
listening to this revelation of profound sorrow,
wild despair, and heavenly consolation.   It was
a glorious memorial of faith and love built into

our hearts.   Never before or since has music
affected me like that.

With young Taubert (then under twenty), who
was almost a daily guest at our house, Felix
quickly established a delightful intercourse.   A
shade of mistrust as to his artistic tendencies soon
vanished before Taubert's frank devotedness.
Felix appreciated his talents; played much with
him; sometimes music for four hands, sometimes
alternately.   We sang the songs of both; they
improvised upon each other's themes; and once
in an extravagant hour they attempted a duet
improvisation.   For some time, by means of
each alternately taking the lead, the other following and accompanying with extraordinary
attention, it succeeded surprisingly well; until
unavoidable and inextricable confusion set in,
and terminated the performance with a peal of
laughter.

A cheerful and intellectual circle frequented
our house at this time; we were blessed with
many dear and interesting friends.   Felix, beloved
and admired by all, found himself in a congenial
atmosphere.   He took great interest in " The

Gipsy," an opera on which Taubert and I were
then at work. When he read my first sketch of
the plot he wrote me a note, illustrated after his
fashion.*

"I wish you joy of the opera, it pleases me
mightily. Read it all through and find it capital;
certain wishes I will confide to you presently,
but the main things cannot be improved. The
close of the third act is beautiful; I must not read
it too often or I shall compose it myself. You
have made a great stride since 'Heiling.'
Hurrah!

"The above sketch is for Felix. The gipsies
are lurking behind the bushes and underneath the
bridge; in the background the seven peaks are
brought in by the hairs, and a sucking-pig is
cooking in the kettle.

"Read this libretto, and do not shiver over it;
but above all do not forget your promise to
give your opinion of it to *no one* but me, and
to read it only with a view to stating whether
you think that with alterations it can ever be

* Here follows a rough sketch of scrub and boulders, a kettle
hanging upon the branch of a tree, and the background closed
in by mountain peaks.—TR.

available, or not. And now farewell; remember
me to the household.

"FELIX M.-B.

"July 10th, 1832."

The libretto mentioned above was Immermann's version of Shakspeare's "Tempest." Unfortunately its availability appeared to me most
questionable; it was not at all operatic; many
obviously musical situations of the original were
altered, and new ones substituted that did not
appear to me to promise much; also the action
was even more dispersed than in the original.

Felix agreed with me. We discussed some indispensable alterations, which, however, Immermann was reluctant to adopt, and thus a new
operatic hope vanished from Felix's horizon.

In the beginning of September, the first numbers of Marschner's score of "Heiling" arrived.
Felix, whose curiosity about it was great, was
immediately called in, also Taubert. Both went
at it, arranging it for four hands, Theresa and I
singing: no four heads were ever more eagerly
bent over one copy. I found many deficiencies

in the music, and Felix had much to do to reconcile me to them. I had yet to make experience of
the great disadvantage under which both poet
and musician labour when they do not work together, and personally interchange their ideas
and intentions. It is particularly unfortunate
for the poet, should he be musical (as every
writer of librettos ought to be), and who, in plan-
ning the pieces of music, has already notions of
their musical effect. If these cannot be imparted
to the composer, he is almost certain to feel dis-
appointed in the way they are carried out. It
was in vain Felix praised this and that musical
beauty; I longed everywhere for a clearer
dramatic embodiment of the situations, with free
expression and unfettered declamation of the text,
and by no means found it throughout.

New numbers of " Heiling," as well as of " The
Gipsy," were continually coming in, played
through, sometimes sung with parts complete, and
propositions for improvements were brought forward—our whole circle of friends taking part in
these trials and discussions; but most of all
Felix, in whom all this operatic turmoil roused

afresh his longing to be concerned in the like. He even reproached me that I made my best things for others and not for him.

"Did I not write 'Heiling' exclusively for you, and did you not reject it ?"

" You have since then greatly improved it."

" Would I not much rather have done so for you ?"

Now it seemed as if he would have gladly composed "The Gipsy," and yet could I have proposed it to him, he would certainly not have decided upon it, partly on account of its similarity to "Preciosa," and partly because of other poetical shortcomings.

His conscientious and critical severity with regard to librettos, and his natural strong impulse to write dramatic music, swayed him in a circle that some evil genius seems to have drawn around him.

About this time an event was approaching, that had long been spoken about, the choice of a new conductor at the Vocal Academy.

Rungenhagen, assisted by a clever pupil of Zelter, Eduard Grell, had filled the post since

L

the death of Zelter. This arrangement had long
subsisted in cases of Zelter's occasional non-ap-
pearance, but had always been regarded as a
makeshift. In the world of musicians, Zelter
occupied but a secondary position ; his compositions and his musical influence were regarded as
highly respectable, but mediocre.* He had been
identified with the Academy from its first begin-
nings, as the faithful helper of Fasch ; and what
with his stalwart person, rough speech, natural
kindness, and the thoroughly able way in which
he had steered this important society through
some difficult passages in its early career, he was
universally esteemed, and his influence counter-
balanced many deficiencies in himself, and a lack
of vitality that was beginning to make itself
felt in the operations of the society.

Would this lack of vitality be likely to be supplied by placing Rungenhagen in authority, an
excellent working musician, but of inferior capacity ? and would the society under him keep pace
with the demands of the time ? Such of the

* He had been a master mason, and entered the art as an
amateur.

members as were concerned for the continuance
of a society which had the highest aim of any
such association in Germany, anxiously pondered
over this question. It was afterwards to be
proved, however, that these members were not
the majority. After a delay of six months, the
choice of a conductor was at last to be made; it
did not appear that an unanimous election would
take place. No one more ardently wished that
the choice should fall upon Felix, than I; it would
keep him in Berlin, and in an independent office
which he would raise to high dignity, and which
would leave him ample leisure to compose. The
matter was much debated between us, as also
with Fanny and his parents. Felix had little
confidence, and would take no other view than
that expressed in his letters from London of the
25th of May, and the 1st of June. He was ready
to assume the conductorship (as he had already
stated to Councillor Lichtenstein) as soon as he
was distinctly chosen, but he would not apply for
it or take any steps to obtain it. He was perfectly right, and I did not attempt to persuade him
to another course, for I placed my hopes in what

Felix had already conceded to Lichtenstein, that he would conduct the society in conjunction with Rungenhagen. I repeatedly urged this plan upon Felix, and though the father shook his head, Felix entered upon it cheerfully, nor did he seem to mind that in the eyes of the public he would appear as second in command. He only stipulated that leave of absence for travel should be granted to him. Lichtenstein promised to support him in this; indeed he was truly desirous to gain Felix for the Vocal Academy; at the same time he was pleased not to appear in direct partisanship against Rungenhagen, with whom he was friendly. So a general meeting of the gentlemen members was called for Sunday, the 17th of August, 1832, at 12 A.M. The minutes of this meeting already showed clearly a division of parties.

The partisans of Rungenhagen brought forward that his long ministry in a subordinate post, and his frequently having acted as proxy for Zelter, entitled him to the first consideration for the chief post, and that it would be base ingratitude in the Academy to set aside these claims.

On the other hand was advanced, most zealously by me, that the Vocal Academy, as an institution of high authority, had a mission to perform— towards itself, in securing the highest influence for its own development, and towards the public, to be identified with the best possible performances at their concerts.   I urged that it was not by patient waiting and careful discipline that a man became qualified for such a task; that it should be a *sine quâ non* with the Academy amongst living conductors to secure the most able; that more than two years ago Mendelssohn had fully shown, in reviving the "Passion" of Bach, and rehearsing it, that of all living conductors he was the most able; that, moreover, he possessed the advantage of youth, which promised the society a long continuance of the same directing influence, and the guarantee of the constantly growing estimation in which his works and his reputation were held.

These representations led to an expression of opinion of the majority, who maintained that the society was but a private association, who met for the pleasure of performing sacred music;

that they had no mission with regard to the public, who were admitted on sufferance only to their performances, and who were free to stay away if they were not satisfied with the operations of the society. Therefore they wished chiefly for a conductor who was personally popular amongst them. Such a one was Rungenhagen, from pleasant old association; such a one, however, Mendelssohn was not, for many reasons, of which his youth was a prominent one; for it was not decorous that so many highly-born gentlemen and women advanced in years should be dictated to by a young fellow. In the course of this somewhat warm debate, I heard said near me, in an animated knot of talkers, that the Vocal Academy, from its almost exclusive devotion to sacred music, was a Christian institution, and on this account it was an unheard-of thing to try and thrust a Jewish lad upon them for their conductor.* A few persons proposed to invite a non-resident artist of eminence to be their conductor, and thus put an end to all strife between the adherents of the rival candi-

---

* It was perfectly well known that Felix had been brought up as a Christian.

dates. Löwe, in Stettin, and Schneider, in Dessau, were mentioned; but the proposition met with little favour. This general meeting ended with a proposition of the directors to select a body of twenty persons to debate upon the matter, and prepare a plan for discussion at another general meeting. I was chosen one of the twenty, and at once proposed my plan of the joint conductorship of Mendelssohn and Rungenhagen. I reminded my colleagues that there had always been two conductors, namely, Zelter and Rungenhagen, so that it would be no innovation, but a new election of offices already existing. Lichtenstein supported me in his usual kindly considerate way, and though the proposition was opposed by the exclusive partisans of Rungenhagen, a committee of three was called to draw up a plan for the distribution of duties in the joint conductorship; this committee was to be Schleiermacher, the Councillor Köhler, and myself. Felix was not averse to this arrangement: he wished to succeed Zelter, as much from reverence for his old teacher (whose wish it had been to have him for successor) as from ambition; and he was not reluctant to believe my assurance

that Rungenhagen would never musically enter
the lists with him, but rest his claims solely upon
his seniority in the office, and the personal regard
entertained for him. Felix's father thought, if
Rungenhagen were not pacified by some other
means, we should have accomplished nothing.

The committee met on the 30th August, at
Councillor Köhler's residence. We allotted all the
duties in detail. Rungenhagen was to be active
and managing director in all matters concerning
business and performances, and the direction of
musical affairs only he was to share with Mendelssohn, who was, however, to be chief authority
in these. We believed we had organized a satisfactory and lifelong office. In four days the
above sketch had been officially drawn up, was
shown to Felix, who concurred in it, and thus it
was sent, the 6th September, to the directors.
At the general meeting on Sunday, the 9th, even
Rungenhagen's adherents expressed themselves
satisfied with the new statutes, provided Rungenhagen himself approved of them.

But this he did not. At the following general
meeting, on October the 2nd, to which the ladies

were also summoned, Lichtenstein stated that he
had called, at the instigation of the directors, on
Rungenhagen, to induce him to accede to the
proposal of the committee, and had met with a
decided refusal. Rungenhagen considered that
he had a right to the post on the conditions
under which it was held by Zelter; and he was
prepared to abide by an election by majority of
votes, a declaration which was well received by
his partisans. After this Felix considered
Rungenhagen as good as elected; at least he was
disinclined to continue a competition into which
much personal prejudice was now beginning to
assert itself. During a long walk which we had
the following evening, I earnestly and unfortunately dissuaded him from his intention of with-
drawing from the contest: his family did the same.

At this juncture we ought to have set on foot
measures for canvassing votes for Felix's election,
but for this we were too diffident and too proud;
the tactics of elections were not yet known in
Germany. The other party, however, managed
more to the point. Rungenhagen had been long
preparing, and now started a train of argument

amongst the lady members, of which the following
was the substance: "We cannot cast out poor
Rungenhagen;" and upon this plea a silent and
compact majority arose in his favour. The
directors gave ample time for agitation. There
were some further committee meetings to discuss
details, and votes were not received till the
beginning of January, 1833.

At last, on the 22nd of January, the election
actually took place, in the evening after the
practice. An officer of rank, who understood the
routine of elections, undertook the business of
recording the names. So long as the majority
was undecided the names were called quietly and
properly; but no sooner had the majority of votes
been declared for Rungenhagen, than the recorder
began to emphasize his name with an offensive
triumph, whilst that of Mendelssohn was mentioned in a desponding, and soon in a pitying
tone, a proceeding which caused frequent laughter.
I was indignant at this, not only on account of
its indecent partisanship, but also because as an
indecorum towards a considerable body of the
members whose preference was registered in

these votes. As none of the directors attempted to stem this scandalous conduct, I
appealed to some acquaintances standing near
me to protest against it. I was overruled,
cautioned not to make a useless disturbance,
and I was weak enough to follow their advice ; to this day I repent that I did not raise
a disturbance.

Rungenhagen was elected by 148 votes;
Mendelssohn had 88, and Grell 4. This result
doomed the Vocal Academy to a long course of
mediocrity, and to serve as foil for the institution
of a new association of the same kind. I could
well imagine the effect these occurrences would
take upon Felix. I was mortified, and forbore to
call upon him until the third day; confessed
myself guilty of excess of faith, and admitted
that without our interference he would have
managed the affair much better himself. He
let scarcely any expression of his annoyance
escape him, but I felt that it would always
rankle in his mind. I was sorry then to learn
that the entire Mendelssohn family, under the
first impression of the election, had seceded from

the Vocal Academy; an error that was now
past recall.

Excepting for the vexation consequent upon
this occurrence, we passed the winter in happy
intercourse with Felix. Much Jean Paul was
read, also Hebel, and plays, with distributed
parts, and we had much music. In his room on
the *entresol*, and during long walks, we had
much conversation, of which a frequently-recurring
theme was his intense desire to have an opera
libretto. His judgment and suggestions were
invaluable to me in my own doings; we met
often in musical circles in Berlin and at his
father's. He resumed his share in the Sunday
performances at home, which had been carried on
by Fanny; for one of these I find the following
invitation:—

"ESTEEMED EDUARD,

"If you will attend our musical performance to-morrow morning at eleven o'clock, I can
promise you two great musical treats: these are,
that you will hear me play my Quartet in C
minor, and that you will hear yourself sing

Weber's Scottish songs.* Therefore come and receive p.p.

" FELIX M.-B.

"Saturday evening (Echo : evening)."

He gave four concerts in the concert-room of the theatre, between November and January. At one of these, for the first time, was performed the " Walpurgis Night," in which he had made many alterations. I was struck by the dramatic effect that the Cantata might be capable of; when I spoke of this to Felix, he said, thoughtfully, " It may be so, try it." " So I will," I answered, " as soon as I have a stage at my disposal."† About this time Felix's pianoforte-playing must have reached its highest point of perfection and individuality. It was not his prodigious and precise mechanism, the sustained energy of his performance, that fascinated his hearers—these were means, and were forgotten;

* Beethoven's ?—TR.

† It has been a stock piece at the opera of Carlsruhe since May, 1860, where Herr Devrient is official director.—TR.

it was his interpretation of the thought of the composer (on which account, too, he only played intellectual music).　In short, he gave musical revelations; through him spirit spoke with spirit. It was to be regretted, with his depth of thought and mastery of form, that he did not oftener extemporise in public; but he used to say, "he had recognized the folly of intending, and even announcing, 'On such an evening and such an hour I shall be well inspired.'"　His playing made a profound and enthusiastic impression in Berlin, but yet not that which it made in other towns.　There was also the circumstance that Liszt had shortly before intoxicated the public with admiration of his dazzling powers, so different in kind.　Felix's compositions, too, did not awake the enthusiastic sympathy in Berlin that greeted them elsewhere; his musical greatness was to be tardily, and even then scantily acknowledged in his own city.　It was a case of a prophet in his own land.

On the 14th of April, 1833, Felix again visited London.　His symphony in A major, some less

important compositions, and his pianoforte-playing
were there received with acclamations. In the
latter part of May he conducted the musical
festival at Düsseldorf, and first introduced
Handel's " Israel in Egypt " in Germany. In this
town, where a flourishing school of painters had
drawn together a number of distinguished artists
into a pleasant and attractive social circle, where
Immermann's zealous activity augured a new
future for the drama, it was not difficult for the
authorities to retain Felix; he accepted the
post of musical director for three years.

His father was present at this festival, and
sanctioned his acceptance of the new office; he
considered it highly important and desirable for
Felix to take upon himself distinct duties and
responsibilities. He returned with him to London,
where Felix still had some concert engagements
to fulfil; but a long-standing complaint in the leg
laid up the elder Mendelssohn, and retarded his
return to the continent till the end of August.   I
received a letter from Felix, dated from the
country seat of his uncle, Horcheim, near
Coblentz, of the 7th September.

" I follow close upon these lines. My father was so seriously ill in London, that, although he is now entirely recovered, I must accompany him home. I shall be able to remain but two days in Berlin, but I hope to spend some time with you and yours, etc."

Felix entered upon his duties towards the middle of September. He was to conduct the church music and the Vocal Association, and had promised his co-operation for the new opera under the auspices of Immermann. He counted upon these duties leaving him sufficient repose for composition, and he felt the society of the many young painters enlivening and congenial to him. I watched with interest his zealous endeavours to organise church music upon a thoroughly new footing, and wondered whether he would succumb to the captiousness and indolence with which he would have to grapple. I had grave doubts, when I considered his excitable temperament, and how entirely he was unused to be thwarted in his inclinations.

I received his first letter under date 30th September, as follows:—

" DEAR EDUARD,

"It is not fair that the first letter I send you from here should contain nothing but a request on a matter of business; but I am now a terrible man of business, have judgments to pass, committees and meetings to attend, of which I dream at night, and which leave me little time by day for writing. As soon as we are consolidated (!) I will write and describe everything; I consider myself immensely well off here.

"My request to you is this : pay a friendly visit to Rungenhagen, for the sake of the following. Five or six years ago Zelter asked me to instrument the ' Dettingen Te Deum ' and the ' Acis and Galatea' of Handel. I did so, gave him the scores, and have heard nothing more of them since ; but I know that they are in the library of the Singakademie. Now I wish very much to have them (they are only scores of the added instruments, not complete ones, and written on my usual upright paper). Indeed, they are necessary to me here, and therefore I wish you to get them for me, and send them as soon as possible by the mail. This is what I

M

should like, and what seems quite natural, as the
Academy does not make use of the scores.   But
as I have no *proof* whatever that they are my
property, and as they are actually in possession
of the Academy, I should not be surprised if
they refused to return them to me : if (as I fear)
your diplomatic powers fail to compass my wish,
at least try to obtain leave to have the supple-
mentary scores copied for me, and have them
copied with all despatch, and finally send them
me (against restitution of costs, with thanks, etc.).
I do not think they could with any fairness
refuse, and it is important to me to have them.
The scores will be easily found ; you know my
handwriting, and must look for them yourself.
Also we translated 'Acis' at the same time
into German; this translation must be somewhere, and I should like to have it if it can be
found. Be sure that you mention that both
scores contain *only my* instrumentation, and are
consequently of no value to the Academy (since
they can instrument their oratorios themselves with
a couple of horns and an old comb and kettle-
drum), and that I wish for nothing but my own

lucubrations. I do not make my request *direct* to the Academy, as I will not ask them a favour (they are sure to consider it as such); therefore I beg of you to apologise for the ' great trouble ' (Earl of Kockburne), and try to get the things for me soon ; I want them here for our winter concerts,* which are going to be very brilliant : you will have to look to it whether your great metropolis will be able to compete with our little town. Our heads are full of raisins (figurative

---

* Through some misunderstanding his score of the " Dettingen Te Deum " did not immediately reach him. He urged again to have it sent, and wrote, " It is most important for me to have either my original MS., or else the score from which the performance was then conducted. I will give my reason for requiring it, which you will approve. In the score of ' Acis ' (which was performed with the announcement, ' Newly instrumented by F. M.-B.') I have found, amongst many good things, several which I could not now endorse, and want to correct before it can pass into other hands, because I consider this matter of re-instrumenting as requiring the utmost conscientiousness. Now it happens that I recollect having done some still more arbitrary things in the ' Te Deum ' than in ' Acis,' and I must expunge these faults (as I now regard them), as I cannot annul the score. Therefore I beg of you to send it me ; I ask it as a great favour. The reasons given above you will of course keep entirely for yourself, as they are intended for you only." I give it to the world, nevertheless, in testimony of Felix's scrupulous sense of duty.

ones), and if all goes well we shall send for
Rellstab or Sobernheim,* or whatever may be
their names, and when these gentlemen are gone
from Berlin it will be all over with your music.
We would like also to have Glasbrenner;†
besides, there is a scarcity of pretty girls.

" Afternoon and the time for digestion have set
in, so I have time for gossip, though I felt hurried at the commencement. I expect the Dirich-
lets ‡ every minute; they were to leave Aix-la-
Chapelle this morning, and will probably remain
with me a few days, after which they will return
to you and bring you all our good wishes. At
this moment the capitals are being placed on the
pillars in front of the new theatre; the mob is
standing around, wondering. If the bill, announcing your first performance in my new opera,

* Newspaper critics in Berlin.

† Perhaps the wittiest of German satirists. His radicalism
exiled him for many years from Prussia, where, however, he
has been lately allowed to return. Glasbrenner is thought
to have been the first to give a literary shape to the biting
wit of the Berlin populace, which was later to culminate in
the " Kladderadatsch."—Tr.

‡ Rebecca had lately married Le jeune Dirichlet, professor
of mathematics.

were but stuck on one of the columns! You must come to the next festival at Düsseldorf, and we will make a walking tour, per steam-boat, and sketch on the road and eat grapes, that are delicious this year—quite glutinous. But now farewell; I must go to the town-hall to see the Oberbürgermeister. Remember me to your ladies most heartily; wish them every joy and happiness, and remember the 'Hofrath' to Marie and Anna and the 'Gräul.' I wish I were sitting at the corner of the table, having a little taste of the dinner. What you write and sing, tell me, and good-bye.

"FELIX M.-B."

The second volume of Mendelssohn's letters shows us how actively he was employed during this winter, and how zealously he worked for the musical improvement of the Vocal Association, and even for that of the painters. He also lent his aid to the so-called model performances, through which Immermann sought to gain the higher public; indeed, throughout a theatrical *fracas*, which the ruder portion of the public made to

express their discontent at the theatrical ameliorations that were beginning to work, he conducted "Don Giovanni" unflinchingly to the
end.* He wrote to me, February 5, 1834, still
fully satisfied with his position :—

"My Dear Eduard,

"Just as I was beginning to write to you,
there arrived your dear last letter, and put me to
shame that I had not long since written to you,
and showed me how vexed you are with me for
my silence. And yet you know that I am not unmindful because I cannot write for a while ; and
that I am not divided from you, though you sit
in Berlin and I here ; and that though the power
of writing were lost to me, we yet would be the
same to each other. It is not quite so bad as
that yet, however : on the contrary, I intend to
make this a very long letter, and if you turn
taciturn and answer not, I shall write again. The
long-promised four-part songs, that I always
intended to write for you, have at last seen the
light, and I have copied them for you for my

* Vide a letter to his father, of December 28.

birthday present.* I intended to pass a very quiet day here by myself, thinking that no one knew of it, but it was not to be; and the day passed in such a whirl, beginning with a morning serenade of the military band, and terminating with a ball that Schadow got up in my honour, and where we danced until half-past two o'clock, that I hardly had time to go home and to make this copy. I wish you to sing these songs

---

* These were three " Volkslieder " of Heine. An altered and, in my and Fanny's opinion, inferior setting, especially of the first, is included in Op. 41. The original melody of the one to which I refer, is as follows :—

Ent - flieh' mit mir und sei mein Weib und ruh' an mei-nem Her-zen aus. In wei - ter Fer-ne sei mein Herz dir Va- ter-land und Va - ter-haus, dir Va - - - ter - land . . . und Va - ter- haus.

sometimes, and to like them much ; this you will
probably not do at the first glance ; you will be
apt to think them confoundedly simple, and say,
' How can one call this composing ?' But never
mind, you may come to it later. How I would
like to hear Theresa's G sharp in the first song!
and Taubert is not to drag the tenor part too
much, nor to sing it too sentimentally ; also,
where will you get the low E from ? Kisting
will have to supply it.* This ought to be a
letter of congratulation on your grey gentleman,†
who seems to have pleased the people uncommonly. A success is a glorious thing, for it makes
one feel a few footsteps farther on, and then one
may go ahead a little and no one will grumble.
But you tell me nothing definite about it, about
the parts, music, or the costumes, or the applause,
or the lamplighters ; just that which you tell me
about the compliments transmitted to you by
Count Redern, from the highest source, does not
interest me half as much as would the above.
And what says my Rellstab—the oracle ? what

* Kisting was the maker of my pianoforte.
† My drama, "Das graue Männlein."

Pythias? Are you to live or not? In Berlin this
is important. Here we have to battle with beer-
bibbers, publicans, and ex-officials, with any riff-
raff, and I must say I prefer our motley public to
your polite *habitués*. What you tell me of your
notion for a novel, 'The Actors,' pleases me
hugely: pray do not let it lie by, but finish it
right off on receipt of this letter, and if you like,
dedicate it to me; at all events send it me.   I
think the idea a very happy one, and I have not
half the power to imagine what it will be that
you have to accomplish it.   You will not forget
to put in a very dissipated, windy, low, good-
natured actor? and you will contrive to show the
splendour and the wretchedness of the stage?
and do not fail to give the public its share, and
tell them for once that a great deal too much is
done to please them.   And do put in an amateur
actor, a fellow with good legs and lungs, who
cares the devil a bit for art, is all self, consequently idolized, and knocks every good thing
out of the field.   In short, get on with it and tell
me about it. Your intention of quitting the
opera, however, is not at all to my liking.   Why

should you, especially as I am going to write for it? I want to keep good people in the trade. Indeed you must sing here during the next spring, and delight our Düsseldorfers. Remember the Bach ' Passion ;' I cannot think you mean it seriously.

"Will you come? It would be charming. I shall write you a letter in the name of the management, humbly inviting you to accept a star engagement, to which you will not reply at all for four weeks; then you will send two lines, to say that you will see what can be done. In short, you would have to come, and afterwards we would make a journey together up the Rhine. We are now rehearsing the ' Wasserträger,'* and every note calls to my mind Eduard Devrient, for it is just as if written expressly for you. Tell me why have you never sung it? Is it because he has a son who gets married? In that case I quote Rokko. Or is the music out of fashion? Jesting apart, you should think over the part and adapt it, of course retranslating it, for performance; get up the choruses and action, and take the credit of having done a good thing.

* Cherubini's opera, "Les deux Journées."—Tr.

The first three bars of the overture are worth more than your entire repertoire, 'Prince Riquet' included in the bargain. Why, you must remain in the opera if only for the sake of having a piece of fun such as this every once and a while, and of letting others share in it. If I were you I would push forward just now the 'Ali Baba' of the old gentleman, and tease the directors till they put it on the stage, where it would fail as it has done in Paris. Pray what is this you write about 'commissioning' me? Do you think that I am 'commissioned' to compose, let us say, a Boot-jack Galop, or choruses to the 'Midsummer-Night's Dream?'* Did they not tell Immermann in Berlin that they 'would make use of me some day?' Am I not languishing my life away ever since in waiting? and when I pull out a grey hair do I not think how it renders me so much more useful for Berlin (twenty-six undeniable years)? And who is to be your Puck—Stawinsky or Blume?† Hofrath Esperstedt must be prevailed

* I had proposed a performance of the play, with music by F. M.-B.

† Two particularly tall and stalwart performers,

on to play Titania. When these parts are filled according to my suggestion, I will undertake to furnish the choruses, and promise to send them to Berlin in 1850, by a travelling acquaintance, to save the expense of carriage. Then however it would still be a question whether the management would accept them.*

"Be not surprised nor vexed that I write you such rubbish; I am particularly joyful to-day at having suddenly lost a most painful ear-ache that has tormented me these three weeks, and made even hearing difficult; the sound of my piano

---

* His antipathy to Berlin found a still more marked expression in a letter dated June, where he answers my request for his music to the "Standhafte Prinz."[1] "As regards my music, you are well aware that I shall always joyfully send you anything of mine, as I do now. As, however, I have a lively desire not to oblige the Berlin Theatre, and as if they were to make an official application for it (which will end in smoke) I should send an official refusal, I must beg you not to give it with my name; otherwise to do with it whatever you like, use it or not. I expect you will be displeased with me for this, but you know I am and must remain a Polish malcontent. The whole affair, however, of your seceding to the drama, and your playing the 'Steadfast Prince,' could not please me more."

---

[1] Immermann's translation of a play of Calderon, for which Mendelssohn wrote incidental music when it was produced at Düsseldorf, that is still unpublished.—TR.

seems quite a new gift.   I caught this ear-ache
driving to a concert at Elberfeld, with a frightful
storm and rain pelting continually into my ear,
and lost it by putting on a blister and letting it
draw for forty-eight hours.   The consequence is
that I am in a very good humour to-day ; not but
that I am generally so, for my life here continues
to be most delightful.   I have good time for work
and study, and utilize it as much as I can.

    " The overture to ' Melusine,' of which I played
you a sketch, has been my first serious piece of
work here : I have finished it.   Then I have
written a somewhat too light, but merry piece for
pianoforte with orchestra ;* now I am at work on
a Scena ed aria for the Philharmonic Concerts ;
after this I shall write a symphony, and in March
intend to begin upon ' St. Paul,' which will be
finished sooner than I had thought.   Tell this to
Fürst when you see him, and thank him for his
great and valuable assistance, for the text is now
most admirable.   I only wish the music may be
like it.   Remember me to Jonas, and to Schleiermacher when you see him, and tell him how often

    * Rondo in E flat, Op. 29.—Tr.

I am here reminded of him. I have also produced some smaller things, several songs with and without words. I must revise my 'Meeresstille,' that is to say, rewrite nearly the whole of the Allegro, as it is, together with the 'Midsummer-Night's Dream' and 'Isles of Fingal,' to be published in score, about which I am exceedingly proud. On the 25th of February I play at a charity concert in Cologne, and on the 26th I am to stand godfather to a child of the musical director at Solingen; on the 9th of March I play at a charity concert in Elberfeld; meanwhile we are rehearsing the 'Messiah' here. There you have my occupations for the winter. The correspondence of Göthe and Zelter displeases me throughout; a total misapprehension seems to pervade it from end to end. I find with books as with people, that they are either suggestions or impediments to me. This book belongs to the latter class, for I always feel out of sorts when I have been reading in it. Do you know that I am making great strides in water-colours? Schirmer comes to me every Sunday at eleven, and paints for two hours at a landscape, which he

is going to make me a present of, because the
subject occurred to him whilst I was playing the
little 'Rivulet' (which you know).   It represents
a fellow who saunters out of the dark forest into
a sunny little nook; trees are all about, with stems
thick and thin; one has fallen right across the
rivulet; the ground is carpeted with soft deep
moss, full of ferns; there are stones garlanded
with blackberry bushes; it is fine warm weather;
the whole will be charming.   In return for my
accepting the picture he is giving me lessons, and
teaching me to use purple for my distances, and
how to paint sunlight.   Lessing has made another
drawing; the subject is the finest he has had yet,
the death of Frederick II. I hope he is going to
paint it, but the fellow is so infatuated with landscape, that it will be difficult to bring him to it.
His reconstructing a drawing, sometimes four or
five times, is remarkable to me; the first is
scarcely to be recognized in the last, but each one
has gained in depth and importance.

" Now I will say something to Felix.

" Boy, what good thing are you about? do you
learn plenty ?   Paint yourself a moustache, and

put on a pointed hat, and then have a run in the garden. Can you draw a tree, or a mill? Tell me this. Give my love to Marie and Anna, and keep well.

"Your Hofrath.

"And now I must make an end; besides, I have nothing more to say. Immermann begs to be remembered to you; he has been quite ill, but is now better, and rehearsing 'Nathan' at the theatre, in which Seydelmann is to act next week. By rights I ought to begin my letter all over again, with 'Dear Mrs. Devrient,' for to send my 'best regards' is altogether too common. I would like to recall myself to her remembrance in an especially nice way, and wish her all that is happy, prosperous, and glad and good, right cordially; and pray that she may not put me down amongst the people forgotten and done with, but quite amongst the living; also I would beg her to come with you next year to the Rhine. Convey this for me; remember me to your sister-in-law, and write. Yours,

"Felix M.-B."

As the time drew near for the opening of the new theatre, he took the greatest interest in selecting the singers. In a letter of the 9th June, 1834, he inquires about a young tenor, whom he had known in Berlin, and continues : " And can you recommend me an efficient young soprano, who has zeal and a voice (she need have nothing else) ? We open on the 1st of November, and I have heavy cares on my mind as chief musical director of Pempelfort." When I had replied that I did not know at the moment of any rising talent, he wrote again on the 28th June : " Although you are unquestionably right in saying that there is no rising singer, still find me one ; the engagement will be quite acceptable." Quite unexpectedly a charming soprano voice and pliable talent was found in the Berlin opera chorus ; she was tried on the stage, and succeeded. I wrote of it to Felix, and received his answer on the 4th July, 1834, with all business-like details.

" DEAR FRIEND,

      " I hasten to reply to your letter of the 26th. As I had not hitherto succeeded in securing

N

a first singer for our stage, and the result of all my inquiries had been unpromising, I am doubly glad at the prospect of our having one recommended by you. Of course I engage her upon your word that she is competent, on which I put implicit reliance, so need not wait for other testimony; I only hope that she has made no other engagement in the interim, and that you will secure her for us in my name without delay. The terms are very fair. As you write that we can have her for 1000 thaler, I offer her this sum for the first year, and the assurance that a free benefit will be added to it in the second year if she remains with us. If she accepts the 1000 thaler, close definitely with her, and write me only a word to say it is settled, and I will send her the engagement to sign. And now, pray, put yourself in my place and find me a prima donna. All that you say of Grosser pleases me, even to the want of style, for it shows that she is young and inexperienced—two of my favourite qualities. If they recall her at Berlin they will be frantic about her here. I would write to her at once myself, but it appears to me more desirable to

empower you (as I do herewith) to treat with
her, and I beg you kindly to do so for me. Will
you offer her, to begin, 900 thaler and a half
benefit? If she consents, so much the better;
and if not, I shall have no difficulty in ob-
taining 1000 thaler for her, and a half benefit
besides. Yesterday was the first meeting of
the directors, amongst which are some of the
best people of the town (the Oberbürgermeister,
Count Spee, etc.). The enterprise is well conducted,
and promises success. We shall probably give
two operas a week, so we shall have enough to
do. I hope you will take some trouble about us;
you might help us in filling some important posts.
We want a first tenor, to whom we are also prepared to give 1000 thaler; also a second tenor,
who might receive 500. Could a promising subject not be found to exist somewhere in Berlin,
say in the chorus? Then we want another
soprano, besides Grosser, at a smaller salary;
and if you could meet with some chorus singers,
tenors and basses, who would engage themselves
for seven months, at 20 thaler per month and
travelling expenses, to see Düsseldorf and the

Rhine, I would have four or five of each. You say that you take an interest in the proceeding, so I need hardly say 'pardon' for troubling you, or 'gratias' for your letter. I will, however, say 'gratias,' nevertheless, for I was and am glad to be thought of by you.

"A two-part song is shortly to appear (at your house). Farewell, and be thanked. Your

"FELIX M.-B."

In my capacity of agent I was initiated in all the sinuosities of theatrical dealings. I did not succeed with the prima donna; and the young chorus singer, who had hitherto been living in the Hasenhaide, where her father was a poor weaver, rushing through all weathers to and from the theatre, attending rehearsals in the morning, spooling cotton at home between whiles, and again attending in the theatre at night, either in the chorus or as *figurante*—this poor girl was now the subject of furious competition between me and the manager at Breslau. Breslau carried off the prize, outbidding me by 500 thaler.

Fortunately I was able to recommend another

talented, though very young girl, the daughter of our chorus-master, Beutler, who proved a valuable acquisition to the new company. On the 2nd August, 1834, Felix wrote :—

" MY DEAR EDUARD,

"First of all receive my hearty thanks for the great kindness you have shown to our theatrical proceedings, and the interest you have taken in them. It is truly delightful to know that there is some one ever ready to lend a friendly hand to every good endeavour; when a thing is once organized and no help is wanted, every one is ready to further it.

"Fr. Grosser will roast in the musical *inferno*, for turning her poetic soul away from us for 500 thaler. How miserable the devils are we know from *Robert le Diable*, and there it will be still worse. I hope Fr. Beutler will be excellent; I have written for the second time to her father about her; to-day we have come to an understanding. Let me again thank you for all—only an instalment, though—for in three weeks I hope to roam in Berlin's plains, in which I want

nothing, be it known, except three or four home-
steads. Yes, indeed, in a few weeks I hope to be
with you, dear old fellow, and I need not say
how I look forward to it. Have some dumplings
with pears ready, and moisten your throstles, for
I shall come famished for song. Old I have
become, too; a genuine provincial music director,
a Philistine, an official; but I have not lost my
merry heart. I shall not be able to stay long, but
we must see each other often, at least every day.

"And let me also thank you for sending the
'Te Deum;' we perform it on the 17th of August
in the church; the choruses are beginning to go
nicely. Ah me! what a deal we shall have to
talk about! amongst other things about your
united petition,* concerning which you do me
wrong when you say that I look upon the
instigators of it as a sorry set. Am I then
proud? am I a Polish count? † are you not one
of them? Have I not always shown respect for
Spontini as a musician (certainly not as a man)?

---

* A petition of poets and musicians for the recognition of
a copyright of ideas.

† This nickname had been given him because of his discon-
tentedness.

yet I could say much about it, but it must be spoken. We shall give 'Hans Heiling' on our new stage in Düsseldorf, and when you come in the spring the bills will have 'Star engagement of Herr Devrient,' and the day after to-morrow the 'Steadfast Prince,' and then there will be sketching; but first let us have our meeting. I have nothing else to say. Good-bye all; love to the 'Gräul,' who must call me 'Hofrath.'

"FELIX MENDELSSOHN-BARTHOLDY, HOFRATH."

Meanwhile I had been prosecuting my search after available talents for the Düsseldorf stage; and when, on the 29th August, Felix came to Berlin, he had only to test and engage his principal and chorus singers. The task was most distasteful to him, as we know from letters written to his family. This coolly considering people and effects, as fitted or not for a special purpose, was foreign to his nature; to him all was personal. The usual wretched manoeuvres revolted him; that a chorister should twice abate his charge, and, after bargaining like a huckster, accept what was offered him at first, he took as a

personal affront, as though the man expected
by such shuffling tricks to attain a greater advantage. He was quite beaten down and full of
bitter feelings towards all mankind after these
bargainings. How would he preserve his equa-
nimity amid similar wranglings that are every-day
occurrences in a theatre? Such things were opposed to his nature.

His stay in Berlin was extended till past September. On his return to Düsseldorf in October
the theatre was opened under Immermann's direction; the month was not over before Felix's
testy excitability exploded, and he threw up his
entire responsibilities.

In this rupture he was not quite so innocent
as he represents himself in the letter to his
mother of November 4; and this he knew, for
he gave a more detailed account to his sister on
the 23rd November; but even that was not a
satisfactory statement of the transaction. To me
he wrote November 26 :—

"You end your letter by wishing me patience
for theatrical affairs. I had already lost it a
fortnight before you indited that wish. I did not

and could not adapt myself to them. My entire time, from rising till going to bed, was taken up with the Düsseldorf theatre, Immermann refusing to take any share in the musical department; whilst he insists at the same time on deciding and disposing of everything in his capacity of director. Moreover, a kind of rivalry was set up between opera and drama, in which I was to represent opera : in a word, one fine morning I got up and remembered that I had come to Düsseldorf for a few years' work, and like Charles the Fifth, I renounced my throne. Since then I have once more begun to write, to compose, to live. Never again in my life will I be a director, and I shall not forget those few weeks. Fie! for shame! to wrangle with a creature for two thaler; to be severe with the good, and lenient with the good-for-nothing ; to look grand in order to keep up a dignity that no one believes in ; to seem angry without anger ; all these are things which I cannot do, and would not if I could. And say I have conquered myself, all is smooth, and we are to have a performance ; by the time the rehearsal begins I feel quite worn out,

and with all this shamming nothing is done.
Then if I come home, and bethink me that I once
had a notion about composing something, it appears to me as if that had been some one else,
and I and my dignity of office appear in my own
eyes ridiculous. No, indeed; this is beyond a
joke. I did think of you much when I threw it
up, and how you would growl over me; but suppose a year and a day went by, and I had accomplished nothing save official dignity and somewhat
better performances in the Düsseldorf opera,
would you not growl then? and so it is better
thus. I go no more to sea, to sea. You might
hand me Spontini's diploma upon a salver at this
minute, I should not touch it; but to be musical
conductor or Kapellmeister I have no objection,
in Kyritz or where you like."

I could read through the lines of this letter
that it was an exaggerated, and not an ingenuous
account of the rupture. The excellent letter of
his father* speaks of it in general terms, dis-
approvingly. I afterwards heard the particulars,

---

* Page 66 of the German edition of the second volume of
letters. Not in the English version.—Tr.

and am bound, in the interests of justice, to say
that Felix was entirely in the wrong. It was
unfortunate that he implicated himself in some of
the business responsibilities, entirely unfitted as
he was for them ; but this fault is rather to be
ascribed to the business-like Immermann, who
ought to have known better, than to Mendelssohn,
who, in his zeal for the cause, too hastily
pledged himself.   The radical error of incorporating a joint administration of opera and
drama in the management of the theatre, Immermann was also answerable for. It was impossible
that Felix should remain in so false a position;
but he should have modified it, withdrawn into his
functions as Kapellmeister, and if his resignation
were inevitable, it should have taken place without
acrimony.   The breach was not brought about by
the theatrical worries, as he represents, but by a
personal quarrel with Immermann, in which Felix
showed a hasty and snappish temper that one
would hardly have suspected in him.

There is no doubt that Immermann was rather
sore about the greater popularity of operas than
plays ; and that contentions about the use of the

company, stage, time for rehearsals, and all other
accessories, arose, which were difficult to adjust,
considering the equal rights of music and acting
in the constitution of the theatre. Immermann
may not always have behaved impartially, but at
the same time it could not be supposed that he
would forego the full use of means to ensure the
best dramatic performances possible. Felix,
however, made some unreasonable demands, in
the tone of one accustomed to have his way in all
things. For example, he required the stage-
manager, Reger, to get up the operas, whereas
Reger was expected to act in the dramas, as
well as to arrange the stage business for them.
Some vexatious letters were interchanged, in
which Felix certainly went farther than to, as he
writes to Rebecca, "condense his expressions, so
that no point was left without retort, and his
independence asserted." He adds, that he has
"done credit to Herr Heyse." I do not think
so; his gentle, rational teacher would not have
approved these letters.

Thus Felix emancipated himself from theatrical
duties, and would, by doing so, have utterly

paralyzed the entire undertaking, for which Immermann had made such great sacrifices, had not the young Julius Rietz, whom Felix had appointed assistant-conductor and violoncellist, shown a remarkable ability to fill the vacant post, and by his youthful zeal succeeded in safely carrying on the opera.

If we could reconcile ourselves to the manner of Felix's retreat, we should rejoice that he was restored to his purely musical duties, and above all to composition. He was busy with " St. Paul;" " Melusine " was produced, and several pianoforte pieces. He was stimulated to write two and four-part songs by the exquisite performance of music of this class at the house of a friend, and he wrote many more songs without words, those delicious pieces in which he gave play to his dramatic aspirations to create musical types—of various moods and scenes,—which will make his name dear in family circles for all time. The two years in Düsseldorf may be called the flowering period of his creative powers.

The offers and correspondence on the subject

of his accepting the conductorship of the Gewandhaus concerts at Leipzig began with the year 1835. His letters* show with what scrupulous delicacy and considerateness towards others he acted. He refused to displace his predecessor, and only when a satisfactory arrangement had been concluded with Polenz (who was a most meritorious teacher of singing, but inadequate as a conductor of the orchestra), would he accept the post.

Meanwhile, he conducted the festival at Cologne, where he was most interested in bringing to a performance Handel's oratorio "Solomon," and the "Morgengesang" of Reichardt. He passed another brilliant season in England, and afterwards visited Berlin. We had some more of the old pleasant days together; he played us the first part of "St. Paul," with which we were profoundly impressed. Felix's manner of thinking and feeling had gradually become so sympathetic and familiar to me, that in hearing any new composition of his I felt as if my own long dormant thoughts had taken musical shape.

* Second volume.

At the end of August Felix left us, and entered upon his office in Leipzig on the 4th of October. Even the first concert, which opened with his "Meeresstille," gave him the most gratifying certainty as to the capacity, zeal, and devotion of the orchestra, of the lively sympathy of the public, and of the general helpfulness of all who could in any way promote his wishes.

To bring these venerable Leipzig concerts, that date as far back as 1735, with Sebastian Bach as conductor, and which since 1781 had been growing in fame by the admirable performances given, always in the old Gewandhaus, under the direction of Hiller and Schicht—to bring them once more to the full glory of possible perfection, and to be regarded as standards of excellence in all Germany—this task, so fascinating to Felix, and carrying with it its own compensation, became henceforth the refreshing source of pleasant labour to him. In the midst of his full enjoyment of this new and congenial position, the heaviest stroke of his life fell upon him, the painfully sudden death of his father, November, 19th, 1835.

He came to Berlin to attend the funeral.
Broken and stunned—as was to be expected in
one who till now had had complete immunity
from earthly care and sorrow—a seeming apathy,
which gave him the appearance of a somnambu-
list, might easily be misinterpreted. No one
could understand the nature of his grief who did
not know the exceptional reverence and affection
that bound the son and the father; who did not
know that his father's approbation was the motive spring of everything he did, nor how
entirely he was ruled by this loving reverence.
He became a little more composed during the
few days he remained in Berlin, but his letter to
Schubring shortly afterwards gives a true and
simple picture of his mental state. " It is the
greatest calamity that could have befallen me,
and a trial in which I must either hold firm or
sink. I feel this now, after three weeks have
passed over me, without the sharp pangs of the
first days, but all the more surely. A new life
must begin for me, or all must cease; the old
life is passed away."

The key to this new life he had fortunately

from his father, who often expressed his anxiety
lest Felix should let the time pass by when he
ought to marry, and thus fail to find the balancing
point of his character, the repose of family life
for his over-excitable temperament. I recollect
the father saying to me, in a conversation about
Felix's fidgetiness about an opera libretto: "I
am afraid that Felix's censoriousness will prevent his getting a wife as well as a libretto."
I laughed at the combination, but he continued
quite gravely, that he was indeed concerned lest
Felix should remain unmarried, like his uncle
Bartholdy, with whom, in reference to this question, he had great similarity.

The earnestness of purpose that every well-
disposed person carries away from the grave of
the honoured dead, the desire to live according
to his wish, could not but arise most strongly in
Felix. The certainty that he would fulfil this
wish by drawing round him family ties, became
clear to him during these ten days; he resolved
to marry, and told his sister Fanny so before
parting.

His quest for a wife was not to be successful

on his return to Leipzig, where however his
artistic powers were fully employed. The public
of the Gewandhaus concerts enjoyed many sur-
passing musical treats in the course of the
winter; works were heard for the first time, and
well-known ones received a new interest from
some new readings, and an always exquisitely-
finished and refined execution. Felix had a
most valuable coadjutor in the violinist David,
a friend of his youth, whose complete unanimity
with Felix's views, to the carrying out of which
he lent his best endeavours, made it possible to
perform Beethoven's Ninth Symphony, in the
February of 1836, in such a way as to make this
marvellous work intelligible even at a first hearing. This winter sufficed to establish him firmly
in the affectionate regard of the Leipzigers,
which remained to him during life, and endeared
their town to him above all others. His contentment was not a little enhanced by his freedom
from business arrangements, which devolved upon
the committee of the concerts. Their president,
the advocate Schleinitz, especially, who had been
chiefly instrumental in bringing Mendelssohn to

Leipzig, was careful to make all arrangements according to his wishes, without giving him the trouble of looking after them himself; and of the more burdensome part of the musical work he was relieved by David. The butterfly wings of his subtle spirit had no heavier weight to carry than himself.

By the end of this winter he had finished "St. Paul," and its first performance took place at the Düsseldorf festival, the 22nd May, 1836. What a sensation this work created, and how dear it has become to musicians, is well known. Since Haydn's "Creation," no work had so planted itself into the heart of the nation.

He did not, however, share the complete satisfaction of the public; and in his constant anxiety to perfectionate his works to the utmost for publication, he made so many sweeping alterations and excisions in " St. Paul," that the parts, already engraved, had to be cancelled. Many a time I heard him say, "I have an awful reverence for print, and I must go on improving my things until I feel sure they are all I can

make them." Felix spent the summer in Frankfort, during which time he laboured to hold
together and infuse new life into the Cecilia
Association, on behalf of his friend Schelble, who
was ill. To do this he sacrificed a projected
tour in Switzerland and sea-baths in Genoa.
But the reward of his generous devotion was not
to be only the good fruits it bore for the association, nor the renewal of his friendly intercourse
with Ferdinand Hiller, who was just then staying
at his native town; here he was to find the
fulfilment of his father's wish. In Cecilia Jeanre-
naud, the daughter of a Protestant clergyman, he
was to find the maiden who was to complete and
calm his existence. Schleinitz had introduced
him to the house of the young lady's mother, who
was a widow, and his relative, not without a
secret wish that one of his cousins might win
Felix's affections. And so it befel. Felix
showed in his dawning affection his characteristic
conscientiousness. He tore himself away, and
travelled down the Rhine, under pretext of
visiting the baths at Scheveningen, in order to
test his passion far away from the magic circle of

the beloved maiden; but he found his heart
so deeply implicated, that he could return with
a good conscience in the middle of September and
betroth himself.

Cecilia was one of those sweet, womanly
natures, whose gentle simplicity, whose mere
presence, soothed and pleased. She was slight,
with features of striking beauty and delicacy; her
hair was between brown and gold; but the
transcendent lustre of her great blue eyes, and
the brilliant roses of her cheeks, were sad
harbingers of early death. She spoke little, and
never with animation, in a low soft voice.
Shakspeare's words, "My gracious silence,"
applied to her no less than to the wife of
Coriolanus. The friends of Felix had every
reason to hope that his choice would secure
repose to his restless spirit, and happy leisure
for thought and work in his home. On his
return to Leipzig, his principal labours were
directing the rehearsals and performance of
Handel's "Israel in Egypt," in which he made
use of the organ in addition to the score; and
reproducing his "St Paul," on the 18th of

March, 1837. After this he went to Frankfort to be married.

He wrote to me during his wedding trip, from the Bavarian Highlands, at Lörrach, the 3rd of May, 1837.

(Vignette of castle on a rock.)

" Wo der Dengelegeist um die mitternächtige Stunde
Auf em silbern Geschirr si goldene Sägese dengelt
(Todtnau's Chnabe wisse's wohl) da sitz ich und schreibe."*

" Perhaps you scarcely remember that I owe my acquaintance with the Allemannic poems to you, and that I have grown more fond of them than of most things, and that they remind me of the time when you used to read them to me. Coming into the neighbourhood, I determined to visit the spot and write to you from thence. But when I considered how long it is that I have neither

---

* " Where the Denglespirit, at the midnight hour, on a silver vessel whets his golden scythe (the boys at Todtnau know it well), there sit I and write." Not quite a correct citation from the popular poem, " Die Wiese." The " Spirit of the Scythe" is supposed to haunt the summit of the Feldberg, from whence the " Wiese," a mountain torrent, descends to fertilise the valleys.—TR.

thanked you for your dear letter, nor answered it,
I felt that I must await some extraordinary
opportunity to ask your forgiveness: the opportunity has arrived, and herewith I do so. I think
and hope that a request to be forgiven, together
with a hearty greeting, written from the Wies-
enthal direct, will be accepted and granted.
You know that I am here with my wife, my
dear Cécile, and that it is our wedding tour; that
we are already an old married couple of six
weeks' standing. There is so much to say and
to tell that I know not how to make a beginning.
Picture it to yourself. I can only say that I am
too happy, too glad; and yet not at all beside
myself, as I should have expected to be, but
calm and accustomed, as though it could not be
otherwise. But you should know my Cécile!
We shall not be able to come so soon to Berlin
as we had intended, certainly not till the
autumn, towards November, for we have still
great plans to carry out before the summer ends.
But no journey that we can make will ever be
more lovely and happy than this one. If you
are startled by the above vignette, you have not

read ' Mutability, a Dialogue on the highroad to
Basle, by night;'* for it is the Röttlerschloss
which we have just driven past, and Brombach
is just below.   I intended to have written to you
from Todtnau, and made my initial sketch there ;
but we arrived so late, and it was so uncomfortable at Ochsen, that I could not settle to write.
In Schopfheim it poured in torrents, which made
us feel a little sad, and so it came that my
writing to you was deferred till sunshine and
good spirits had set in here.   I have sketched
Todtnau for you, thus.

(Vignette of a village, enclosed by hills.)

" *Frankfort*, 15*th of May*.   Arrived yesterday,
and carried this letter about thus far.   I think I
ought to begin another one, but as it is you will
best see our stirring life and its changes; and I
must send the drawings, for we have spent the
whole day, as far as weather permitted, upon
them, and vied with each other in making them.
Cécile has the advantage of me in the figures, and

* The name of one of Hebel's poems.—Tr.

I excel in the planks and houses. And now that I feel some amount of repose, I come to the question I should have put at first: What are you doing? How are you and yours? Merry, and happy, and contented? Do you think sometimes of me, who am now no longer a Polish malcontent, although for ever sundered from Berlin? Whilst I write to you, and vividly recall you and my family to mind, I cannot bear to think that our life is so divided, whilst we so truly belong to each other; but as it is so, no doubt it is for the best.

"Those are kind, pleasant words you say to me about my 'St. Paul,' and I am particularly pleased that you have liked it with piano accompaniment,* for then you will find it very different with orchestra, which in many cases cannot be represented on the piano; indeed, I should not like to hear the whole oratorio with piano. But even with the orchestra, there are only a few numbers which quite satisfy me, and express exactly what I wished to convey. I intend soon

* He alludes to a performance that took place in the summer drawing-room at Mendelssohns'.

to compose another, in which I hope to succeed better. I suppose you shake your head, and say I ought to write an opera; but this may not be, for I cannot find one. Indeed, I almost despair of it, and when I see the state of the theatre at present, I am consoled, for it must either be improved in the next few years or become something horrible; in either case I had better wait; I have time enough. Meanwhile there is no fear of my becoming a big-wig, though I should write six oratorios, for between whiles I cannot help also writing things for the piano, songs, etc., in all of which I should not take such delight if I had not means in plenty to produce them. Moreover, I will not allow you to shake your head too hard, since you have deserted the standard of opera, and of the world-commanding Spontini (end of an hexameter), who is certainly a curious prince. Enough of this : tell me what has become of your novel about actors. Do you refuse me all intelligence because I am lazy? I am almost afraid, yes, nevertheless I add my present address. Do make use of it, and let me have a letter about you and yours, and your doings. Regards to

your wife and family, and farewell! farewell,
write once, and think often of your

"FELIX MENDELSSOHN-BARTHOLDY."

After the performance of "St. Paul" at the
Birmingham festival, where he received honours
such as had never yet been accorded to him, he
took his young wife to her new home in Leipzig,
where both were most cordially received, and
where Felix passed the winter in happy activity.
He did not bring his wife to Berlin until the
end of April, 1838.

How often we had pictured the kind of wife
that would be a true second half to Felix; and
now the lovely, gentle being was before us, whose
glance and smile alone promised all that we could
desire for the happiness of our spoilt favourite.

Cecilia remained with the family of Felix,
whilst he went to the festival of the Lower Rhine.
This year he succeeded in inserting a psalm of
Sebastian Bach's in the programme, which had
been refused him the previous year. The Festival
Committee were afraid of the stern old master,
but Felix's persevering efforts won the day.   He

had set himself the task of restoring the great old masters to honour and appreciation; and beyond a question the present day owes it to Mendelssohn's continuous struggles that these foundation-stones of musical art are held in just veneration.

Felix returned to Berlin, where he found the family circle more harmonious and cheerful than ever through the addition of Cecilia; we, however, experienced the proverbial falling off in our intercourse after his marriage. The alacrity with which Felix the bachelor came to us was not continued by Felix the husband; besides, I was having a house built for myself at that time, which took up much of my attention. In short, though we met often, both at my house and in his family, though we discussed the sorrowful theme of the opera in many a walk, we parted in August, each of us reproaching ourselves for having let many an hour slip by unenjoyed.

All Felix's friends had now to submit being placed in the second class of his regard, yet how warm and lively this regard always remained, a letter will show that he sent me on the death of

our daughter Anna, aged eleven years ; it is dated
the 2nd of October, 1839, Leipzig.

" MY DEAR FRIEND,

"I heard of the heavy, grievous loss you
and your wife have sustained, in a letter from
home ; you will be sure that I have been daily
with you in my thoughts since then, and mourned
with you for the loss of your dear, beautiful child,
because you know how unchangeably I am your
friend, and have a share in all the joys and all the
pains of your life. Tokens of sympathy and
words of comfort will not be wanting to you at
this time, but how little power have they to
assuage ! and when written, even less than when
spoken. Still, if it be but for a moment, whilst you
are opening this letter, I should like to disperse
your thoughts a little, and remind you of one
who in every distance remains near ; one who feels
the shock that has been given to your happy and
united family life as acutely as if he dwelt amongst
you still. If your wife had but surmounted
the first days of bereavement, and were able once
more to take comfort in all that Heaven has

bestowed and spared her, and you again restored to the power of working! It takes time
before this is possible, and yet it is a healing
power. But the true consolation can only come
from above; may it soon, very soon, be granted
to you and your dear wife.

" I wish you would procure a short leave of
absence and come to Dresden ; there have a look
round the picture gallery, and run up by train
to us, and spend a little while here. We have
much to tell each other, and though you may feel
little care or interest in everything else just now,
yet the change of scene might have a beneficial
effect. Here you would hear a great deal of
music, and much of it, I believe, you would like ;
the finished way in which we play the symphonies
of Mozart and Beethoven, I know would please
you. We have not very much music during the
summer ; it begins with the autumn, and from now
to November is at its height, when all are assembled, and both executants and listeners have
gathered fresh love and power in the long recess.
By New Year's day there is almost too much of
it, and when spring returns one feels quite ex-

hausted and surfeited with music, so that a stop
is very welcome. These conditions have by
degrees moulded my arrangements. During the
six winter months I am overwhelmed with concerts, visitors, and no end of worldly concerns, so
that only seldom, when the impulse is quite irresistible, I can steal any time for my natural work.
But in the summer months I have delightful
leisure; a musical festival or two makes but a
short interruption, and gives pleasant occasion for
travel. So long as God spares me wife, child, and
self, in health as hitherto, there is not a wish I
could form, only gratitude for the great happiness
that is accorded to me.

"Speaking of my work, no doubt you will be
asking about an opera. There is not one in
progress yet—you know why. But as I am
never idle, and write as much as I possibly can,
without having words for operas or oratorios at
hand, and as I take great joy in other things,
you must really forgive me, and let me have my
way. Meanwhile you have not written me your
novel about the actors yet. Now, farewell for
this day, my dear friend. All I say is meant

equally for your wife : best remembrances to all
your circle. Be always as ever towards your

"FELIX MENDELSSOHN-BARTHOLDY."

A sojourn of five weeks that he made in
Berlin, in May and April of the following year,
1840, with his wife and child, gave us satisfactory
confirmation of the grateful and restful contentment which the above letter breathes. They
came to cheer his mother during the absence of
the Hensels, who were gone to Italy. I saw
much of Felix at his family's, and also at our new
house in the Thiergarten, not far from him. He
was then busy compiling the text of " Elijah,"
having relinquished the plan of treating the subject of St. Peter as a counterpart to St. Paul. He
had not given up the search after an operatic
subject, and discussed the matter with Gutzkow,*
whom he met at my house, yet he was less intent
upon it than formerly; he had arrived at a
period of life when the claims of the present
moment found a fresh and glad response in him.

* Author of " Uriel Acosta " and many less known plays, and
of the novel, " Die Ritter von Geiste," popular in spite of its
inordinate dimensions.—TR.

His pleasure in travelling was scarcely indulged
this summer, few of the distances being as yet
accessible by railway, to lessen its fatigue. He
took Cecilia to Frankfort, went to the Rhine,
then to Birmingham and London, and was
punctually returned to Leipzig to celebrate the
fourth centenary of the invention of printing, on
the 25th of June. On this occasion his Symphony-
Cantata, which has been called "Lobgesang"
(Hymn of Praise), was performed in the market-
place, with ample appliances and profound effect.*
In the middle of July we saw him again in
Berlin, on his return from the festival at Schwerin ;
and in August he presided at a grand organ
concert, the receipts of which were the first
instalment towards the monument of Sebastian
Bach. To his unceasing and valuable labours of
this year must be added his successful efforts to

---

* This is not quite exact. The composition performed in
the market-place was a "Festgesang" for double male chorus
(Mendelssohn conducting one and David the other) and brass
instruments. This was on the 23rd, for the uncovering of the
statue of Gutenberg. The Hymn of Praise was first given
in St. Thomas's Church, with reference to the same solemnity,
after Handel's "Dettingen Te Deum" on the 25th.—TR.

attain an increase of salary for his faithful
Leipzig Orchestra, and his initiating the musical
conservatorium there. He had the gratification
of repeating his "Lobgesang" in honour of the
kindly king of Saxony, who visited Leipzig, and
to receive rich tokens of the king's gracious
appreciation. Felix had the satisfactory consciousness that he had founded the conservatorium
at Leipzig, incorporating into it the funds of
Blumner's bequest.

The growing felicity of his married state, his
anxious solicitude to avert every interruption
of it, his full contentment with life, to which was
only wanting the having his family and oldest
friends to share it with him—a letter he wrote
to me in the November of this stirring year bears
witness to. He wrote it, having missed my visit
to Leipzig, being himself on an excursion to
Dresden.

"DEAR FRIEND,

"I am heartily sorry to have missed you
here; when they told me how you had been
taken through our rooms, I felt I would rather

have lost the whole Dresden journey than the
pleasure of showing you all myself. But unfortunately you were only staying here for a short
time, too short to have admitted of any real quiet
for us together, especially as you were outward
bound, when one is restless till one has reached
the journey's end. This I felt very poignantly
in my last journey to England. I undertook it
in fear and trembling, and with a heavy, heavy
heart. As soon as I was on the Thames I
thanked God humbly for having brought me
safely to port; and with unutterable joy I
returned home, and found my wife and children
well and blooming.

"Were it but granted to me to share and
enjoy so many blessings with my friends of
former time, who are after all the true and only
ones! My friends and acquaintances here know
me only with such or such a beard, and that is
not, after all, the distinguishing mark. But this
is too good to happen, and in Berlin, from what
I can notice, the prospects of music are so dreary
and comfortless, that one ought to be glad to be
out of it. I suppose in life something must

always be wanting, and how can I be thankful
enough for so very much?   *   *   *
Good-bye for to-day, dear Devrient, and continue
to love me. Remember me to your dear wife
and the children, and think sometimes of your

"FELIX."

We cannot but feel a deep sadness in seeing
from this time forth a continuous agitation,
excitement and annoyance creep over his happy
and fulfilled existence, his blest and prosperous
career, which sinister influence was to lay the
germ of his premature death.

The new reign of Frederic William IV. of
Prussia, amongst many other excellent projects,
was to inaugurate the institution of a universal
school of art, in which, under the title "Music
Class," a conservatorium for the study of music,
a school for music and acting were to be included.
Felix was thought of as director of this institution, and correspondence was opened on the
subject in the beginning of September, 1840, on
the part of his brother Paul, and the Secretary

of State, Von Massow. The second volume of
Mendelssohn's letters gives the clearest information about this transaction. I have but to add
my own part and experience in it. It was not
from the Mendelssohn family only that I drew
my intelligence of the affair. My pamphlet,
"Ueber Theaterschule" (on dramatic art), to
the production of which Alexander von Humboldt incited me, perhaps with a view to the
projected conservatorium,—had received the
approbation of the king, and elicited his promise
that he would not be unmindful of the matter:
at Christmas time this was more clearly expressed
in a letter from Count Redern, from which it
appeared that the plan for the conservatorium
was fully matured. The king had granted an
additional 12,000 thaler to the expenses of the
institution. Cornelius was to be at the head of
the pictorial department, Mendelssohn to represent that of music; a section was to be
built for fine arts; the schools and classes in
connection with the Royal Theatre were to be
amalgamated with this, etc. Alexander von
Humboldt confirmed the expressed wish of the

king, and dilated upon the grand results to be
expected from the reformed academy, and stated
that the king counted upon my conducting the
dramatic section of the musical "class." All
this sounded fair and hopeful, but between plans
and results lay the task of carrying out. Some
zealous, some well-meaning, also some apathetic
or inimical persons were called to this task. All
were inexperienced in the practical working of
such projects, and went about it with official
circumlocution; and under these conditions
Mendelssohn was expected to act as professional
adviser and planner.

Felix had a presentiment that something was
here expected of him that went against his nature,
and this partly explains his impatience in the
whole affair. To judge of him rightly, one must
take into consideration his own position, and the
state of matters in Berlin at the time.

He had brought the Gewandhaus concerts to
a pitch of perfection which placed them at the
head of all symphonic performances in Germany,
and made them looked up to as the highest
standard of excellence; the conservatorium at

Leipzig was fairly established. Felix was bound
in double duty towards both institutions, and
with the certitude that in both he laboured for
the true advancement of the art of his country.
This great field of labour was now to be given
up; he was to descend to the artistic level of
Berlin; and this without having a fixed course of
activity prescribed to him, or the musical means
at his disposal being either equal or willing to
co-operate with him. He had no hold but on the
intentions of the king, the carrying out of which
depended on too many diverse influences to make
it much more than an airy vision. A pecuniary
question it could not be with him, for the death
of his father left him in affluence, besides which
his talents secured him a handsome income. It
was expected from him that he should combine
and organize the musical elements at hand, overcome all opposition, and create a musical atmosphere in Berlin that should be worthy of the
intellectual metropolis. It must not be overlooked that upon this he was also to stake his
youthful reputation.

It is no exaggeration to say that musical art

was in a state of decadence in Berlin, notwithstanding that the great masterpieces were heard
and prized by the public. Several societies, each
numbering upwards of a thousand, met for the
study of vocal music. Music was heard in every
family circle, in every assembly, and the military
bands helped to spread a taste for good music,
down to the lower ranks, by their performances
at public gardens even of Beethoven's symphonies.
No city exceeded Berlin in musical aptitude, but
it had no leading and directing influences. Its
most important musical performances were without artistic significance; they were mediocre.
This assertion cannot be refuted by bringing
forward the ministry of Spontini, then drawing to
a close at the Royal Opera; it was altogether a
period of false splendour, ruinous to the spirit of
German music, of which Spontini had not an
idea. The violent contrasts in which he sought
his effects, the startling shocks of his *sforzati*, in
fact all his effects, calculated to tell only on the
nerves and senses of the listeners, could not but
demoralize his orchestra. To this was added, that
the perfect precision and control for which his

conducting was famous, ceased when he no longer held the *bâton*. Moreover Spontini managed the choice of his proxies (for he conducted only what he was pleased to call the *grands ouvrages*, namely, his own operas) in such a way that the entire remainder of the *répertoire* should be so executed as to serve for foils to the performances given under his own direction, which alone were to be identified with any excellence. Under these conditions no intellectual progress and honourable ambition was possible to the orchestra, and thus it happened that the execution of symphonies at this period was entirely void of higher insight or charm of reading, and produced but the most inadequate effect.

The Vocal Academy, too, was no longer able to take the lead in choral singing; its glories were soon superseded by the newly-instituted Domchor, and the Vocal Union of Stern assumed a higher social importance.

Such was the condition of things when Felix, at the earnest solicitations of his mother and family, and Herr von Massow, came to Berlin in the spring of 1841, to consult, and prove on the spot whether anything for the advancement of music was to be achieved here by him. He was thoroughly in earnest about making the trial to accomplish an important work in his father's city, and it had been during life his ardent wish to live in the midst of his family and old friends. He had declared his intention, both to the authorities of the Gewandhaus concerts and of the court of Saxony. But no earnest intention of his ever quite effaced his continually-recurring suspicion and repugnance to the Berlin circumstances, nor his attachment to Leipzig, nor finally his distaste for officially-conducted business. With a divided mind he came to Berlin; this was not unknown to his friends at Leipzig; they did not believe that Berlin would offer him whole measures, and they knew that Felix would never accept half measures. At a serenade that was brought him on the parting day, when his song, "Es ist bestimmt in Gottes Rath " (it is decreed), was being sung, Felix stepped amongst the singers and heartily intoned the concluding words, "auf Wiedersehn;" every one believed that they would "meet again." David was deputed to

direct the concerts, and the construction of the
conservatorium was quietly to proceed.

When Felix came amongst us in the beginning
of May, and informed us of all particulars as
matters stood up to that time, I could not but
approve of the position he had taken. He could
have nothing to do with vague or half measures ;
he must have full authority, or retreat. Nor
could he accept the title of Kapellmeister,
and, like Cornelius, Rückert, and Tieck, on a
salary of 3000 thaler, devote himself exclusively
to the service of the new government, and be
only at the disposition of the king; his young
and productive energies would never admit
of this. Still I fondly hoped that a great and
satisfactory result would be arrived at, if only
the expressed wishes of the king could be carried
through, in spite of the circumlocution of his
officials. In this spirit I and his brother once
more urged our views upon him, and he listened
favourably.

But the very first great conference quite upset
him again. The matter was ·not treated simply

and with directness, but wrapped in formalities
and generalities; the Council of Education, also,
who were to hold the distribution of funds for
his department, held ominously aloof. Two long
hours did we debate after this occasion in the
shady walks of the garden, trying to allay his
rising and growing dislike to the whole affair.
I endeavoured to impress upon him that the view
he took of the matter was not a just one, in so far
as he expected too much from others and not
enough from himself; that he accepted the task
of founding a conservatorium, and at the same
time expected it to be handed over to him spick
and span, before he could make up his mind to
accept the direction of it; that he required immunity from all unavoidable trials and troubles
in bringing means and ends together, from the
animosity and uncongeniality of persons and
circumstances, etc.; in a word, that he would
only do just what was sympathetic to him, and
nought besides. I maintained that he had no
right to expect practical arrangements from
persons unversed in the subject, and exhorted
him for once to overcome his nature and go into

a matter not congenial to him ; to take upon himself " odiosa," to have patience with ceremonious-
ness and pedantry, and to put forth all his energy
to bring about the result. I said how he was
the only man in all Germany who could accomplish the happy plan of the king; that this great
chance for the progress of German music, once
lost, might never occur again, and that the great
responsibility rested on him. To all these fine
things Felix wanted not for replies, and I silently
agreed with him that it was hard to fight against
the dominant conditions; that to do so required
peculiar powers, which Felix did not possess in
the least. However, he promised that he would
do his utmost.

He handed in his memorandum for a music
school to be instituted in Berlin, which is to be
found in the second volume of his letters,* and
told me that he had bound himself towards Herr
von Massow (who acted in the matter from the
most noble and sincere motives) to remain one
year, in order to bring matters to a clear issue;
this was a hopeful prospect.

* Page 258 of Lady Wallace's translation.

In ten days, however, I again found him, after a second official conference, quite beside himself. He told me that " he would not stay here, but from Leipzig, whither he was called immediately for the adjustment of sundry affairs, he would send in his resignation. He felt he was not the man for Berlin, for people who wanted to have him without being able to make use of him." Of the honours and rewards offered him he spoke with the utmost disdain, longed only to escape from the official atmosphere, to live again amongst people who had some soul, some enthusiasm for music, away from this narrowness of dominion and mediocrity.

I knew that nothing could be done with him whilst this storm lasted; I knew he was not in the wrong, so I could do nothing but try to soothe him with generalities. I went to him the following day to renew my homily; that he should not, spite of all his suffering, think of leaving before the termination of his promised twelvemonth, and that he would for ever repent if he left a great service to art unperformed. I could have spared my wisdom, for Herr von

Massow, against whom Felix had already taken the field, held him down to his given promise; and so he departed, to return in August for a twelvemonth.

Meanwhile he was appointed Kapellmeister to the King of Saxony; whilst in Berlin it was attempted to withdraw this title from him, which had been already offered.* Herr von Massow succeeded in reconciling matters again, for the compositions the king required from Mendelssohn during the coming winter could not be brought out without the authority conferred by the title. Most inconsiderately they wounded him, and more yet was done to irritate his sensitive nature.

On our return from the sea-side we found Felix, with his wife and children, in high spirits; he was full of good intentions that were soon to take shape in cheerful work. By command of the king, Tieck had gone to Potsdam, and the first result of the intercourse with his new master was the project to revive one of the classical tragedies.

* Page 261 of Lady Wallace's translation.

Tieck proposed the " Antigone " of Sophocles for the experiment, as being nearer in feeling to modern Christian associations than any other; and because, through Donner's recently-published translation, it was practically accessible. All doubts as to treatment of the choruses were solved by the king giving them to Mendelssohn to set to music, who, deeply impressed with the grandeur and beauty of the poem, conquered Tieck's scruples and procrastinations so well, as to have the work fully in train by September. The musical treatment of the choruses was much discussed between us; every praise and every censure that the composition afterwards met with was then foretold and weighed; Felix did not enter upon his task without the fullest consideration. The first suggestion was to set the chorus in unison throughout, and to recitative interspersed with solos; as nearly as possible to intone or recite the words, with accompaniment of such instruments only as may be supposed in character with the time of Sophocles, flutes, tubas, and harps, in the absence of lyres. I opposed to this plan that the voice parts would be intolerably

monotonous, without the compensatory clearness
of the text being attained. In their essential
features, especially in the lyrical and contem-
plative passages, and those apostrophising the
many-named God, and by the involved structure
of their sentences, these choruses are intelligible
to an attentive reader only by careful study; an
expert declamatory actor would scarcely render
their sense clear to the public by a mere recital;
how could this be hoped for from a chanting
chorus? Verbal distinctness then being unat-
tainable by a chorus, no musical feature ought to
be sacrificed for the sake of it.

Nevertheless Felix made the attempt to carry
out this view, but after a few days he confessed
to me that it was impracticable; that I was
right in maintaining the impossibility of making
the words clear in choral singing, except in a few
places that are obviously suited for recitative;*
that the chanting of a chorus would be vexa-
tiously monotonous, tedious and unmusical; and
that accompaniments for so few instruments

* The passages, " But see, the son of Mencetius comes," etc.;
and " See, Hœmon appears," etc., are examples.

would give so little scope for variety of expression,
that it would make the whole appear as a mere
puerile imitation of the ancient music, about
which after all we knew nothing. He concluded
therefore that the choruses must be sung, as the
parts must be recited, not to assimilate themselves
with the usages of Attic tragedy (which might
easily lead us into absurdity), but as we would
now express ourselves in speech and song. The
form and purport of the ancient poem, the spirit
that still lives in it, would unconsciously tend to
make of its representation something quite
different from any drama of our day. With this
I fully concurred, and Felix set so vigorously to
work, that in a few weeks he played me sketches,
and by the end of September nearly the whole
chain of choruses was completed. Besides my
delight at the beauty of these choruses, they confirmed me in the certainty that Felix's genius was
eminently dramatic. They not only gave the
key to every scene, the expression to each
separate verse, from the narrow complacency of
the Theban citizens to their heartful and exalted
sympathy, but also a dramatic accent soaring

far beyond the words of the poet. I allude particularly to the dithyrambus that occurs between
Creon's attempt to rescue Antigone and the
relation of its terrible failure. This song of
praise really consists entirely of glorifying appeals
to Bacchus, and its dramatic application lies only
in the verse :—

> " She was its pride,
> Who, clasping the Thunderer, died;
> And now, seeking its lost repose,
> We pray thee to come and heal its woes.
> Oh hither bend,
> From thy Parnassean heights descend."

To raise this chorus to be the terrible ˙ turning
point of the action ; to bring here to its culmina-
tion the tension excited by the awful impending
doom ; to give this continually gathering power
to the invocation, " Hear us, Bacchus!" till it
becomes a cry of agony ; to give this exhaustive
musical expression to the situation, marks the
composer to have a specifically dramatic gift.
And this is betokened no less in the melodramatic
portions. The idea of adding rhythmical accompaniments to spoken words may have been

suggested by a few well-set passages in the music to "Faust" by Prince Radziwill. It is to be regretted that the public is scarcely able to appreciate how exquisitely Mendelssohn has done this, since the representatives of Antigone and of Creon are seldom sufficiently musical to enter completely into the composer's intention, besides that in two passages of the accompanied dialogue of Antigone, the words are not correctly set under the music.*

Felix took the utmost pains to identify his music with speech in these passages. He made me declaim them to him with full dramatic expression, when he would stipulate for so much rhythmical extension as his music required; and when we had determined, after manifold lengthening and shortening of accents, what the declamatory expression was to be, then he fixed that

---

* As nearly as these passages can be identified through the translation, the first occurs page 41, where the words "Will set for ever," should be spoken to the D D D C♯, which now stand after those words; and the second is page 43, "Like the ivy's," which should be spoken with the four quavers B E G♯ B. No English interpretation has ever approached such exactness.—Tr.

of the accompanying music ; but for his fine
sense of dramatic vitality, these melodramatic bits
would never have become the masterly things
they are.

And thus Felix's wish, for once to "supply" a
great work on commission, was granted, and the
work supplied with the greatest despatch. After
Tieck's first reading of "Antigone," on the 9th
and the 14th of September, we deliberated on the
manner of setting the choruses. He showed me the
sketches of them on the 25th and 26th; we
discussed about the melodramatic passages, which
he decided on the 28th. The choral rehearsals
began in the first days of October ; the piece was
read on the 10th October, Felix accompanying
the melodramatic scenes on the piano. He proceeded so rapidly with the instrumentation, that
our first stage rehearsal could take place on the
22nd, in the concert-room of the theatre. The
orchestral platform was on this occasion used as a
Logeion, and the place for the public was filled by
the chorus, as though it were the Greek *orchestra*,
and by the instrumentalists.

The result upon me of the first rehearsals was

disappointment; I was impressed as by an
artistically-conducted archæological experiment,
and felt sorry that the magnificent music would
not be fully prized through it. But at the
general rehearsal in the new palace at Potsdam,
when I saw the actual Attic stage represented,
the chorus, sequestered from the actors in their
orchestra, became a distinct impersonation.
Through its symbolism of the double stage, I
then fully understood the purport of the Greek
tragedy in its grand conventionalism ; and fired
by the simple majesty of the poetry and the
loveliness of the music, I ascended the steps of
the *Logeion* in the *rôle* of Hœmon.

We had two more rehearsals on the following
day, the evening one in the presence of the king,
and the performance itself took place on the 28th,
before the court and all the invited celebrities of
art and science.

It produced a very great sensation. The deep
impression that the revival of an ancient tragedy
could produce in our theatrical life promised to
become an influence ; it has purified our theatrical
atmosphere, and it is certain that to Mendelssohn

must be ascribed great and important merit in the cause.

Although the learned, of whom each expected the ancient tragedy to be put upon the stage according to his peculiar conception of it (which would, of course, be totally different in every case), might find the music too modern—too operatic,—in fact, not sufficiently philological, it is undeniable that Mendelssohn's music has made the tragedy of Sophocles accessible to the sympathies of the general public, without in any wise violating the spirit and aroma of the poem, but rather lending it new life and intelligibility.

The venerable Böckh* said of it that he found the music perfectly in harmony with his conceptions of Greek life and character, and with the muse of Sophocles; that Mendelssohn had made such use of modern art-appliances as were compatible with the character of the choral passages and the thoughts they contained; and that the excellence of the music was decided by the noble

* The great classical *savant,* whose exhaustive labours in the field of Greek literature would give especial weight to his approbation.—Tr.

and dignified impression created by the work as a whole, which must set aside all scruples of the antiquarian conscience, especially as no antiquary would be able to supply genuine Greek music in the place of it.

A juster reproof was that violence had often been done to the measure of the old verses in order to accommodate the exigencies of modern rhythm. But this disadvantage was inevitable. Whoever reads the choral verses with a competent musical faculty, will confess that no music could grow out of them that would correspond with modern requirements whilst their actual form was preserved. In short, Felix had every reason to be satisfied with the success of his work, with the warm appreciation of the king, and with the reverent enthusiasm of his friends; and he was satisfied.

Much was, however, yet wanting to give him confidence in the condition of things in Berlin. Although he had taken a house, opposite to that of his family, which his wife did everything to make into a home, he secretly kept open a pos-

sible retreat to Leipzig, where he went for a
visit after the performance of "Antigone," on the
6th of November.   He was received with acclamations, conducted three Gewandhaus concerts,
and in a circle of friends directed a performance of
"Antigone" at the piano.   By the end of the
month he returned to us, and we rejoiced in his
inspiring co-operation during the winter.   My
dramatic lectures, the completion of my play,
"Treue Liebe," greatly furthered by his critical
counsel and judgment, its production, and that of
Werder's "Columbus," which excited great interest amongst our friends; to all these doings his
keen and lively participation lent a peculiar
charm.

The concerts given by command of the king, in
the concert-room of the theatre, began the 10th of
January, 1842, with a performance of "St. Paul,"
at which the choruses were sung by a numerous
company of amateurs, selected by the committee
apointed by the king.   It created a great effect
and profound impression, which the public, however, did not share.   This was the moment when
the pianoforte-playing of Liszt had intoxicated

the public to the point of aberration; they had no ears for earnest music. Some disagreeables had also recurred at the rehearsals, such as had already shown themselves in the orchestra during the rehearsals of " Antigone." Sarcastic jokes and observations were made, even Felix's instructions were questioned, which drove him to be angry and hasty, whereas a chill and impartial severity, which his office of Kapellmeister entitled him to exercise, would have been far more fitting.

But all this was not likely to instil a better opinion in him of the Berlin orchestral players, nor to reconcile him generally with Berlin; once again he declared decisively, to Baur and myself, that he would return to Leipzig. Nor would he listen to our imploring him to remain only until the Conservatorium should be started, of which musical Berlin stood so sorely in need, and which would never take shape without his help. He said that he felt quite unequal to official business, that he did not believe anything would be done except endless unproductive parleyings, whilst Leipzig would complete its Conservatorium safely and without noise. He felt himself useless here;

both people and institutions were so distasteful to
him, that he believed it to be a duty to quit a
spot which he felt to be so ungenial.

Meanwhile he proceeded with his concerts,
conducted a performance of "St. Paul" in the
Vocal Academy in February, and close upon it
one at Leipzig of "Antigone." The first representation of this work on the Berlin stage was not
until the 13th April, Felix conducting ; thus long
the authorities had hesitated to bring the work
before the general public. The impression it
made, however, was so decidedly favourable that
within three weeks six more representations of it
were given ; its solemn and religious tone delighted and edified even the lower strata of the
public.

During this winter in Berlin Felix completed,
besides smaller compositions, his so-called Scottish
Symphony (in A minor). On the 25th of April
he gave his last concert, which included the
"Hymn of Praise," and some pianoforte pieces.
But the reception given to him was not cordial ;
and to his formal application about the structure
of the Conservatorium, he received a reply which

consisted in mere vague assurances, and left him
without certitude as to the future ; he was therefore glad to go to the Düsseldorf Festival,
where he was received with open arms. In
London he was greeted with storms of applause,
not only at his own concerts,* but at others where
he appeared only amongst the audience, where
the cry, "Mendelssohn is here!" caused the entire
public to rise from their seats, and ministers of
state to take precedence in giving him marks of
their enthusiastic esteem. Finally he went back
to Leipzig, where the entire city received him as
a beloved relative. Was it then to be wondered
at that he returned to Berlin in October with the
sole intention to release himself from his engagements there ? And yet the king so fully recognized his value that quite recently he had
admitted him into the limited number of Knights
of the order *pour le Mérite;* but he was powerless
to make good his position.

The plan to found a Conservatorium was cast

* Herr Devrient must mean concerts in which he was engaged, since he gave none himself in England. The whole of
this passage seems a little overwrought.—TR.

aside as a worn-out toy, and with it faded all my hopes of a dramatic school for Germany. Felix's published letter to Herr von Massow, of the 23rd October, 1842, another to the king, and his account to Klingemann of an audience with the king, gives sufficient information about the changes that were now proposed in his ministry. He returned to his post in Leipzig, with a half-salary of 1500 thaler, for compositions which the king would commission him to write. The first were to be music for Racine's "Athalie," for Shakspeare's "Midsummer - Night's Dream," and "Tempest," and to Sophocles' "Œdipus in Colonos;" moreover, the king appointed Mendelssohn General-Director of church music, the functions of which office were yet to be regulated.

In the midst of this renewed and liberated activity occurred the sudden death of his mother, of cerebral paralysis, like that of the father. With her was lost the parental home, which still had remained to him after the father's death. Felix felt this most acutely, yet he mourned for his mother with incomparably more gentleness, for his intellectual dependence on her was not so

great as it had been on the father, also his life
was now more centred in itself. Work was
again his great solace in grief, and just about this
time much was expected from him, for the pro-
spectus of the Leipzig Conservatorium was published on the 16th January, 1843. The staff of
teachers named in it was a splendid one : Mendelssohn for pianoforte and composition, Moritz Haupt-
mann for harmony and counterpoint, Robert
Schumann for pianoforte and composition, Ferdinand David for violin, Becker for organ, and
Polenz for singing. Shortly afterwards Moscheles
was added for pianoforte, and after the death
of Polenz, Böhm for singing, besides assistant
teachers. Six free scholarships were endowed,
and the institution was solemnly inaugurated on
the third of April, 1843.

Thus without grand speeches and conferences,
without his being wearied with business details,
Mendelssohn's influence had created a good and
important institution, one which has not yet, notwithstanding the severe loss it has sustained in
Mendelssohn's premature death, been surpassed
in Germany.

Meanwhile an altered set of tasks had been traced out for him in Berlin. He was to direct the Royal Orchestra in the symphonic performances, which had been instituted by Taubert with the happiest result; the authorities were also deliberating on the way to bring his activity to bear upon church music. In May he came again to Berlin, in company with David, to attend more conferences, which resulted in nothing practical.

I wrote to him stating my views of these questionable new propositions, also about an interchange of visits; about my giving some performances at Dresden, and sent him the text of an opera which had been written by a gifted poetical friend at my instigation. He answered me on these points the 28th of June, 1843, from Leipzig.

"DEAR EDUARD,

"Best thanks for your letter, for the enclosure, and, best of all, for your promise to come and remain some little time with us. This last is so very much the most important that I would rather write nothing else, but to ask you to come and stay as long as you possibly can. One or two days is the very least that you ought to think of sparing us from your journey. You will find plenty of amusement in the little nest for a couple of days; half a day is of no use at all, but to say 'were it but more.'

"I will then return you the opera libretto; much of it I like, above all the singable, throughout musical verses, also the subject of the lovespell, which in my thinking would give scope for a fine earnest composition. But, as a whole, the form of an opera in five acts, with spoken dialogue, is not congenial to me. I should not like to compose an opera with dialogue, which I would even prefer to see eliminated from shorter operas, but in an opera of five acts I should consider continuous music essential. A second objection proceeds out of this first, which makes it still less desirable for me, this is, that there is too much in it; there are so many effects that I think one will destroy the other; thus, the opera might just as well conclude with the fourth act, as with the last, or the first might be left out, &c., &c. Not but that the same objections, and more, might be applied to most of the librettos set in the present day. But——

"Atterborn's 'Isle of Happiness'* contains no material for an opera, according to my thinking. Magic and enchanted fountains are not sufficient to make a subject operatic; that which does, the simple, noble, all-pervading human element, I did not find in it, although there are some fine poetic passages.

"Ever since I began to compose, I have remained true to my starting principle: not to write a page because no matter what public, or what pretty girl wanted it to be thus or thus; but to write solely as I myself thought best, and as it gave me pleasure. I will not depart from this principle in writing an opera, and this makes it so very hard, since most people, as well as most poets, look upon an opera merely as a thing to be popular. I am aware that popularity is more essential and natural to an opera than to a symphony or oratorio, pianoforte pieces and such like; nevertheless, with these even, it takes time

* The poem had been recommended to me as likely to furnish matter for a libretto, and I had requested Felix to read it.

R

before one stands sufficiently firm to be above
all danger of being misled by external considerations, and this leaves me hope that I may yet
write an opera with joy, and the good conscience
that my principle has not wavered. I see you out
of humour, saying, 'The moral of all this is that
he will write no opera at all.' Oh, do not say so!
You are the very man who ought to help me to
one, if you chose! Ah, if you only would! for
art has the same place in your heart that it has
in mine, and we have always had a perfect understanding in things about which one never
hopes to come to an understanding with other
people. Has nothing yet occurred to you, which
regardless of all else might become a true work
of art? have you no new subject? The other day
I thought that if five or six pieces of Shakespeare
could only be put into composeable verses, they
would be just the thing. Do you agree with me?
Perhaps 'Lear'? or 'Faust'? I always return
to the latter.

"Now, in conclusion, a word about the Berlin
affair. Above all, thousand thanks that you
have not reserved your sincere, friendly opinion;

it only vexed me that you seemed to find it so
difficult to tell it me that, at the close of the
letter, you are still considering whether you ought
to send it. I confess to you that the whole matter
has become indifferent to me. If they insist on
my going to Berlin, I will go, because I have
promised it; but if they place the least difficulty
in my position or course of life there, I will leave
again in six months, and not return. My remaining
here these nine years will sufficiently shelter me
from the charge of instability; and the Berlinese
are so in the habit of abusing all and everything,
that they are by no means implicitly believed in
Germany. I do not think anything will come of
the plan about the symphonies; should it be
carried through, contrary to my expectations, it
will be the affair of those who are arranging it;
I have warned and disputed enough, and my conditions are sufficiently explicit. I cannot withdraw entirely, because of my given promise.
More when we speak.

"Come and stay! Remembrances to your
family.

"Your FELIX."

We did not meet, because he was recalled to Berlin to fulfil some wishes of the king. The negotiations about his new office had, as he tells his brother,* caused him so much vexation that he almost fell ill. Notes of the conference of the 10th of May had been sent to him, to which had been added six or eight stipulations which entirely cancelled what the conference proposed to effect. The fact that upon his protesting, these stipulations were withdrawn, could only exasperate him the more, as it showed them to be only a tentative whether he would let them pass. Of this he wrote to me on the 31st of July, and that the end of all the annoyance and scribbling was that he must go yet once more to the king, then at Berlin: "I had settled everything for the trip to Dresden, and looked forward to it so, and now I must see Zahna and Luckenwald instead, which is bad enough, therefore pardon," &c.

The duties that were now being arranged for him, intersected offices already existing, were sure to meet with opposition, and would have been found impracticable. For instance, that the Royal

* Page 336 of Lady Wallace's translation.

Orchestra was to be placed at Felix's disposal for the concerts which he was to give by command of the king, was a vexatious hindrance to the arrangements of the general Intendant; whereas it was not to be expected that Mendelssohn would be in any way subservient to arrangements of Herrn von Küstner. The office that was being arranged for him by persons who knew nothing of art practically had no distinct field of operations, it touched upon all, interfered everywhere, and caused general discontent, which at last must fall upon Felix.

Meanwhile he conducted the Domchor at a solemn celebration of the thousandth anniversary of the founding of the German empire, at the beginning of August, after which he was again called to Leipzig, then back to Berlin, to conduct "Antigone" at the new palace at Potsdam on the 19th, which occasion served for some discussion on the "Midsummer-Night's Dream," for the rehearsals of which he returned at the beginning of October.

He was leading the life of a musical man of business, whilst his composing and conducting really required repose and concentration, and all this with inward repugnance and struggle, which could not but tell hurtfully upon so finely-strung a temperament.

The only bright spots in the Berlin transactions were the commissions of the king; this time it was the "Midsummer-Night's Dream" that formed Felix's relaxation. When he brought it with him, at the end of September, completed, some incongruities were perceptible, in consequence of his not having written it with the scenic requirements constantly in view. Tieck also had neglected some points that had been settled upon; thus he divided the piece into three acts, certainly not without good reason, so that the night in the wood might not be interrupted; but Felix did not know of this and had composed two *entr'actes*, according to Schlegel's division (Nos. 5 and 7), that were too lovely to be suppressed. Some expedient was to be found to bring in these pieces in the course of the act without dropping the curtain. This could be done with the *agitato* in A minor (No. 5), to accompany Hermia's seeking after her lover, especially if filled by the actress with grace and variety; but with the *notturno* in E major (No. 7), the long contemplation of the sleeping lovers was rather a painful effort, and Tieck's escape from the dilemma, by pushing forward some pieces of scenery to screen the lovers, was rather coarse and stagey, and of doubtful effect.

The beauty of the composition made people indulgent to these shortcomings, no less than with the song of the fairies (No. 3, A major), because it does not fulfil Titania's "Sing me now asleep," and is less a slumber song than a merry round of the fairies and their sprightly "Good-night" wishes through the wood. Though the exact dramatic expression may be wanting in this piece, the whole remainder shows in its musical treatment of the wondrous poem such fulness and variety of power in the representation of character, as to prove undeniably Mendelssohn's dramatic vocation. The originality of his portrayal of fairy life has become typical; all later composers have, in similar subjects, followed in his footsteps.

The rehearsals of the "Midsummer-Night's Dream," in which I was to play Lysander, were begun on the 27th of September, 1843, in an upper story of the royal castle, in the so-called Hall of Elizabeth,—we were here, because with the daily performances at the theatre, the scaffolding, three storys high, on which a portion of the action was to take place, in imitation of the old English stage, could not be put up. On the 5th of October Mendelssohn brought in the orchestra, and on the 10th and 11th we already rehearsed at the new palace at Potsdam.

As Felix and I were together in the railway as well as at the hotel, we could talk over many an anxiety about the success of the undertaking, and find many a fault with the scenic arrangements. But these practical stage considerations so rekindled Felix's old desire to write an opera that, amid all the fatigues of the rehearsals, he continued the never-ending theme; he wanted an opera—and I was to find him one. Not only at our meals, but into the night, from one bed to the other, we discussed and tried to fashion something out of a subject I had recently proposed to him from the "Peasant's War."

The "Midsummer-Night's Dream" was rehearsed again in the new palace on the 13th and 14th; on the evening of the last, as with "Antigone," in the presence of a large assembly, by royal invitation. Many of Felix's friends had come from Leipzig for this evening's rehearsal, amongst them David and Hiller, with whom he was very intimate in Leipzig. All were full of the liveliest sympathy and admiration of the music.

In the total impression produced by the performance, with its scenic realities and full-grown fairies, it had to contend against the airy conceptions as to how it should be, which every reader of Shakespeare brought with him. It took some time, and repeated performances in Berlin, of which that of the 18th was the first, before the public was at all favourably impressed with the representation of the "Midsummer-Night's Dream," with all the shortcomings of the stage. Mendelssohn's music conduced mainly to bring about this favourable impression, and his music, apart from its dramatic application, won its way much more rapidly into public sympathy than did that to " Antigone."

For the second time the expressed wish of the king, and the solicitations of Herr von Massow, induced Felix to reside in Berlin. At the beginning of December, 1843, he was settled in the house of his parents; Cecilia ever quietly content to be wherever it pleased him. In the course of the winter he conducted, alternately with Taubert, the symphonies performed by the Royal Orchestra, played his pianoforte compositions, conducted the Domchor, on several solemn occasions " Israel in Egypt" in the garrison church; he gave a new impetus and attractiveness to Fanny's Sunday performances, and brought much joy into our circle. At the same time it was not at all congenial to him to appear now here, now there, as a star conductor; to feel that he could exercise but an ephemeral influence upon the various institutions with which he was brought into momentary contact, and to know that after him all would sink again to the old level. He was also annoyed to find himself acknowledged and received, by virtue of his titles and orders, in quarters where,

the previous winter, he had met with nothing but
coldness. Soon also began the misunderstandings
and misinterpretations of his conduct with reference to the king's commission for him to set the
choruses of the "Orestia" of Æschylus. People
would not or could not conceive how a composer
might have an invincible diffidence to enter upon
so peculiar a task. The heart-burnings extending
over years, till March, 1845, that were to grow
out of this, are shown in the second volume of his
letters.

Indeed, by the commencement of the year 1844,
Felix had another fit of Berlin panic, and we con-
doled with each other upon our respective vexations, as I was no less dissatisfied with my artistic
position there than he. He repeatedly declared
that he must quit Berlin. In spite of much unavoidable ill-humour, Felix had never been more
full of cordial sympathy for me than during this
stirring and eventful year in my life; in this he
rivalled our friend Werder, and shared our domestic cares as though they were his own. He
took the keenest interest in the correspondence
which paved the way to my being transferred to

Dresden; he would see every letter, and took every expression of mine sharply to task, that I might mar nothing by oversight. He used to say he envied me an appointment which would assure me a regular and productive course of work; and when he came to me one day in March, I having just received the news of my engagement as chief director in Dresden, exactly according to my own stipulations, and asked him whether he advised me to relinquish my native town, the society of my friends, and my twenty-five years' service to a graciously-disposed king? he answered, "There can be but one question in the matter: this is, have you sufficient trunks and cases to pack your things? if not, I will lend you some. Dearest Eduard," he added affectionately, with the old drawl, and stroking my head, "the first step out of Berlin is the first step towards happiness!"

Whilst he thus regarded Berlin as a prison, it was impossible that his stay in it could be permanent; it was scarcely natural that his grateful sense of the king's favour and graciousness should retain him, where every other influence was crush-

ing his life and powers. No good result would
accrue to the king under these circumstances ;
meanwhile Felix was maturing a plan by means of
which he hoped to liberate himself without offend-
ing the king. He told me that he intended to
ask for a year's leave of absence to visit Italy,
that he would during that time reside there
with his family, and thus by degrees dissolve
his tie, not to the king, but to Berlin. It
did not come to this ; but as I parted from
him on the 10th of April, 1844, when he was
on the point of taking his family to Soden,
and of then going to England, the conviction
became strong in me that the turmoil and
hubbub of Berlin had given a manifest shock
to his delicate and sensitive organisation, and,
together with his cheerfulness of temper, the
fresh and spontaneous flow of his ideas was
dimmed and weakened.

My residence at Dresden, from June, 1844,
brought with it a great change in our intercourse,
which must be now restricted to mutual short
visits interchanged at Dresden and at Leipzig,

in the event of his returning to the latter town. Meanwhile he wrote to me from Berlin, where he was winding up his affairs, under date the 25th October, as follows:—

" DEAR EDUARD,

"Hübner shall not return to Dresden without taking with him my hearty wishes for your lasting welfare. All I have heard of your new home has given me the greatest pleasure : first I received your own letter, and then I spoke with many ear and eye-witnesses who were full of your praises, which redound no less to the praise of the Dresdeners ; then Werder came amongst us and gave us all particulars—all that I longed to know. That your contentment with your present lot will not diminish, but go on increasing, I believe ; and I wish you nothing but health for you and yours, continuance, unchangeable change, or the reverse—you know, &c. God speed !

" How I should like to witness all the pleasant and nice things you are brewing out there ; let me hope it will not be long before I do. If it is at all practicable, I shall carry out my original intention, and pay you a visit in the course of November.

" My position here has been modified during the last few days quite according to my wishes. I shall continue to stand in relations with the king as a composer, for which I shall receive a moderate salary, but of all connection with public performances here, and necessary residence in Berlin, which have so long tormented and weighed upon me, I am happily quit. I hope shortly to return to my relations at Frankfort, and often come for a cursory visit to Berlin, but never again to stay. By this means I shall have even more enjoyment in seeing my family than is possible whilst living in this indescribable place, and thus all will be as I have wished, and as only the happiest conjunction could have arranged it. More of this when we meet.

" My wife and children are better, thank God! though the youngest continues to be weak and ailing; please God, the coming spring may benefit him as much as did the last, then he will be as well again as, Heaven be praised! the others are.

Thousand kind things to all your family, till our happy meeting.

"I have another opera in my head that you must make for me.

"Yours,

"FELIX."

At the beginning of December I saw him for a few days in Dresden; the King of Saxony wished to hear him play some things on the piano, he then intended to resume his post in Leipzig, and in the meantime, needing rest, to return to his family at Frankfort, and occupy himself exclusively with composition. One standing subject of conversation,—the opera,—came up again; he had been thinking of the subject of Loreley, which I had proposed to him, but had as little found the dramatic treatment of the legend as I had. We neither of us then knew the romances of Brentano, which Geibel afterwards made use of. His letters show that even in his tranquil life at Frankfort the longing for an opera haunted and disturbed him.

"Frankfort, the 26th April, 1845.

"Have thousand thanks, you dear Eduard Devrient, for your letter; these three weeks I have had a firm intention to write to you, and now you have anticipated me! how glad I am to hear your good, pleasant news, and that you continue to like Dresden, and that I have been a true prophet. And I prophesy further, that your satisfaction will go on increasing, since you are now over the first shock, in which I believe I shall be found no less correct than before. May Heaven only give perfect health and peace to your home! this is the soil upon which all earthly felicity must be built for such as we, for art is as closely bound up with it as soul is with body. Here, too, things are mending again, God be thanked! our little child gets better day by day. Next month we are going to take him in the country (in the Taunus to Soden), and the doctor thinks he will there lose all symptoms of his ailment. The child had been given up, and we thought recovery was impossible; so fancy our joy! We others are well, and enjoying the spring-time, in the midst of this lovely scenery,

s

with all our hearts.   I have been again reflecting much upon the furry chestnut-buds, but I do not yet understand quite how such a tree grows. Botany explains it about as well as thorough bass does music. In the last-named I am busy; I feel, for the first time this many a day, what it is to live quietly and work, and what happiness it brings to have not only one leisure hour, and now and then a leisure day, but a long series of leisure days before one for work; then I am really happy, and enjoy both the work and the days, music, my wife and children, and myself, which is only possible when, as here, there is no hurry-skurry.

"I have written several new things; the last is a trio for piano, violin, and cello; begun another symphony, and some vocal things; a new book of songs without words will also appear in the course of the year, and six sonatas for organ. The choruses to 'Œdipus in Colonos' also are finished, and I hope they are far superior to those of 'Antigone.'   But as you say, above all things, I should write an opera; sometimes I long for it exceedingly. The day before your letter arrived

I had been writing to a friend, that I often reproach myself, particularly when (as during this
winter here) I hear new German operas; I then
feel as if it were a duty for me, too, to lend a hand
to the cause, and record my vote in score; and
it is a duty, although it does not depend on me
to perform it.   It appears that I do not possess
the talent to arrange a plot into scenes; this is
the one thing wanting; verses are easily to be
procured, even I could write bad ones; this is no
difficulty.   Since I have been here I have daily
employed my leisure hours in reading, and endeavoured to contrive a plot, and put it into shape.
The whole of Zschokke, all sorts of historical
works, &c., I have ploughed over with this intent,
but nothing comes of it; I have not the capacity
for doing it.   I wanted to tell you this these
three weeks, and add a despairing sigh and a
prayer for help!   I have the firm faith that you
could do this thing, and I cannot but think that
with your continual supervision of the *répertoire*,
which must be constantly occupying your thoughts,
how many subjects must be always revolving in
your mind!   And if you would but say to one

or another: 'Hold! this might make an opera '—
then if you would write out the plot on two pages
of a letter, my wishes would be fulfilled! More
than the scantiest plot, that is to say what is to
happen in each of three acts, more than this is
not needful; I should not even like more than
this, I repeat to you. If I have this, I have the
opera, for I can recognize and trace it out myself
from a few broad strokes; but I cannot make
them myself. How I should rejoice if it was you
who helped me to this! I know no resident
poets; I could not make an acquaintance with a
direct view to this; besides nothing would come
of it; my experiences have been too disappointing,
and I am determined I will never set a bad
libretto (*i.e.* plot). Do see what you can do for
me. The development of the plot, as I said, I
will get done for me, or do myself; but the
ground plan! there's the rub! It should be
German, and noble, and cheerful; let it be a
legend of the Rhine, or some other national event
or tale; or let it be a powerful type of character
(as in Fidelio). It is not to be Kohlhas, or Bluebeard, or Andreas Hofer, or the Loreley, though

there might be something of all these! Can you make me a verse about all this? I forget, I do not mean a verse, but a plot.

"I want you to help me!

"And now many kind messages from me and my wife to you and yours, and to your sister-in-law. I hope to see the 'Verirrungen' next week; I only know it from reading, as I was unable to go to the first two representations. They say it is not well given, but the 'Senatum populumque Francf.' seems nevertheless to have relished it highly. Give my cordial greetings to Bendemann, the Hübners, and the Franks, and continue to love your

"FELIX M.-B."

Another letter shows how the thought of an opera continued to torment him.

"Baths of Soden, near Frankfurt, a. M.,
"July the 2nd, 1845.

" DEAR EDUARD DEVRIENT,

"I have been longing for your reply to my former letter, but it has not yet appeared. Can you not soon send me one? I have been feeling during these last days as if in a few

months there would be the score of an opera
written by me in readiness, and as if bright
national choruses and all sorts of sweet thoughtful
songs would be rivalling each other in it.   Then
it occurred to me that the chief thing was yet
wanting; the thread on which to string them ;
and it is for this I write to you this evening, and
ask 'what cheer?'   Have you not found anything yet for me? has nothing beautiful and
German occurred to you as suitable for music ?
Say!

"My family is, thank God! well, and I hope it
is the same with you and yours.

"Ever thine,

"FELIX M.-B."

If one reviews this constant urging and praying
for an opera libretto, extending as it did over a
period of more than ten years, it may appear un-
friendly in me that I did not long before then
procure him one.   But on a closer consideration
of his requirements in the matter, it will be seen
that, though they were in semblance so small, yet
in fact they were very great.

Nothing but a plot sketched out upon two pages, but a sound plot, formed upon an appropriate and promising subject, and just this is the chief and only thing for a dramatic poem. To give such a sketch into strange hands is a doubtful thing, for the effect of each scene must greatly depend upon the way in which it is worked out in detail. How would the second worker find the exact clue of the original intention and follow it out? The method of proceeding proposed by Felix was very precarious. And what demands he made on a libretto! I had no expectation of satisfying them. Besides Heiling, I had proposed to him the legends of Bluebeard, of King Thrushbeard, the Musk Apple (Bisamapfel), the Loreley, a plot of my own, of two friends, whose estrangement and reconciliation was to unfold itself in Germany, in the Italian Carnival, and in the Swiss Alps; then Kohlhas, Andreas Hofer, and an episode of the Peasants' War; in each of these I had done my best to bring the musical points in relief, yet not one could win his entire sympathy. Besides which, my present duties, to superintend the performances of plays, made the field of opera seem more remote, and my occupations in Dresden left me little leisure. Nevertheless I had resolved, merely to show him my good intentions, to put together a plot of some kind as soon as ever I could.

With the Saxon court, too, Felix almost got involved in disagreeables.

When he had freed himself from his Berlin thraldom, the King of Saxony manifested a wish to hear Felix often in Dresden, also to secure his occasional assistance as conductor. The Minister von Falkenstein, who had negotiated Felix's return to Leipzig, had conducted the matter from the side of the Saxon court with the characteristic delicacy which marks all its proceedings with Mendelssohn. The pecuniary emolument and the precise functions of his office were to be fixed by Geheimrath von Lüttichau, who could not but be desirous to draw Mendelssohn to Dresden. But he had only vaguely intimated his intentions when Felix passed a few days in Dresden in December, 1844; and when he again visited that town, the 26th of August, 1845, Herr von Lüt-

tichau missed seeing him. All this Herr von
Lüttichau related to me when I saw him, on the
11th September, at his country-house in Pillnitz.
He, of course, wished to have the exclusive nego-
tiation of the matter, feared Herr von Falkenstein
had failed to mention the essential points, that he
harboured the wish to attach Felix to Dresden;
indeed he entered eagerly into my project, hastily
thrown out, to transfer the Conservatorium to
Dresden, and to connect a dramatic school with
it,—for he understood that so comprehensive an
institution in Dresden, in the midst of its manifold
artistic influences, might become of high importance to Germany. He requested me to undertake the mediation with Mendelssohn for filling
an office here, and I opened a correspondence
with him on the subject on the following day.
I wrote to him:

"Lüttichau has informed me of the negotiations
with you, for he thinks that through a friend the
differences may be more easily smoothed, which
he fears may have arisen through Herr von
Falkenstein. He regrets much that he did not
see you in Dresden, and fears that the fragmentary

nature of his letters to the minister may have left you dissatisfied, especially in regard to your relation to the resident Kapellmeister, which he most distinctly desires to model according to your wishes. Although he is sorry that you have withdrawn from direct communication with him in favour of the minister, he has the lively wish to do everything to win you for Dresden; he says that the king looks forward with peculiar pleasure to the realisation of this plan. So he has commissioned me to open an easier way to further the matter: this is for you to tell me roundly what you wish and what you do not like. What he told me about the possibility of combining a career for you here with that in Leipzig, has to me the appearance of a medley, out of which you must select what you choose; in the meanwhile all is open before you, and you would in any case have a freer field than you had in Berlin. But I will not seek to persuade you, as I did three years ago, and have sufficiently repented since.

"Only say to me, dear Felix, how and if I can be of use in this delightful plan. You know," &c.

He replied:

"Leipzig, the 15th September, 1845.

" DEAR EDUARD,

"Many thanks for your kind lines, which were sent after me to Berlin whilst I was returning hither, and which I received here only yesterday. I would have preferred to answer by word of mouth, but I cannot, for the fourth time in a fortnight, absent myself from home, much as I would like personally to clear up the misunderstanding which seems to be the motive of your letter. That there is a misunderstanding is apparent to me when you say that Herr von Lüttichau regrets that I had addressed my correspondence about my future appointment to the minister, &c. But this I never did. It is Herr von Falkenstein who has wanted me to return to Leipzig these three or four years, who by word and by letter has made me repeated propositions on the subject, which I could not accept on account of my engagements at Berlin. Herr von F. wrote to me (without my in any way leading to his doing so, as you may suppose) to Soden, on the 5th of June this year, and asked me whether I was now in a position to return to Leipzig. To this I naturally had to reply as I had to his subsequent letters. But from what you know of all the circumstances, you are aware that I was not enabled to treat either with him or with Herr von Lüttichau, but that I could only give a simple reply to whatever was asked of me. As Herr von Falkenstein wrote to me, in the king's name, that I should return to my former office, and assured me distinctly that my (though almost nominal) engagement in Berlin would be no obstacle and should on no account be relinquished, and as, at the same time, all he said of the business part of the arrangement quite coincided with my wishes, I have returned here, and begun to feel at home and set to work. Beside my former duties, which I resume, Herr von Falkenstein mentioned that I would be expected occasionally to play the pianoforte before the king; Herr von Lüttichau made me a similar gratifying proposition last winter, to which I answered that I was most willing in my *private capacity* to contribute to any musical performance before the king, as well as elsewhere in Dresden, although I could not engage to assume any official capacity there, which would certainly be *hurtful* to the musical conditions in Dresden, as they are known to me. As Herr von Lüttichau seemed quite of my opinion, I thought, what Herr von Falkenstein wrote to me on the subject was but a new proof of the kindly regard entertained for me by Herr von Lüttichau, and felt inwardly grateful to him for it. But what the misunderstanding may be that has occasioned your letter, what wishes I am supposed to entertain (of which, I am sure, I know nothing), is not clear to me ; and, as I said above, I wish I could ask you all about it by word of mouth, for it is quite lame writing about these things; I have got to the end of it. Yet I cannot leave home at present; therefore, pray communicate from this letter as much as you think expedient to Herr von Lüttichau, and in any case tell him how truly grateful I am for his constant and friendly kindness, and that he gives me a particular proof of this when he occasions you to write to me, which kind boon I acknowledge and appreciate with all my heart.

"Ever your,

"Felix M.-B."

It was easy to perceive from Lüttichau's communications and this letter, that the affair was very immature as yet on both sides, and that it had better bide its time. For the moment it was put off till we could meet personally.

Meantime I sought to make Felix's dramatic talents still better known in influential circles than they were through the choruses in "Antigone" and the "Midsummer-Night's Dream;" I got up a private performance of his operetta, which created a great sensation, and the silent wish that Mendelssohn might be induced to live here. I was enabled to write to him about it quite satisfactorily, when I asked for his signature to the petition of the poets and composers of Saxony, to the Landtag, for intellectual copyright. He replied the 11th December, 1845 :

"MY DEAR EDUARD,

    "I ought to do nothing else this day but ask your forgiveness for not having written to you a fortnight ago. But, indeed, it was impossible. You know I would gladly have done it; but the 'trouble' in which the time passed on

this occasion in Berlin,—through the two performances of 'Œdipus' and 'Athalie,' besides
the attendant rehearsals, court concerts, business
matters, and social obligations,—was so great
that for days I had not a minute to myself, and
could not even think of writing a letter. To-day,
for the first time, I can quietly look over my
letters that have accumulated during these weeks,
and am not a little ashamed to find your dear
handwriting amongst them! Be not angry with
me! It is too late now for signing the petition,
of which your letter speaks; but it is not, and
will never be, too late to thank you for all the
love and goodness that the other letter contains.
From old times you know that nothing in the
world can happen to me that gives me so much
pleasure as when such as you say pleasant
things to me about my music; that this is dearer
and more important in my eyes than everything
that is called success and appreciation; that I
have no higher ambition than to merit such contentment and such pleasant words. Be thanked,
then, that you have written to me thus!

" And if anything further should occur to you

about the 'Peasant's War,' write it to me; and
may it occur to you soon! I am now again
greatly inclined towards an opera. Jenny Lind
so urged me to write her one, and I should so
like to compose something first-rate for her, and
she would sing it capitally, and that would be
nice. See that you help me to something! You
will be calling me Cato, and this kind of ending
to a letter a *denique censeo*. It is not unlike it;
but Carthage was destroyed at last, &c., &c.

"Thousand greetings to all, from your

"FELIX M.-B."

When the occurrences of February, 1846,
which accompanied my retirement from the
management, made some days of change and
repose necessary to me, I went to Felix at
Leipzig, and with him found all I needed,—insight, sympathy, counsel, and encouragement, and
all in his tender and kind way of imparting them.
Of these helpful qualities he had lost none.

I found him living in opulent comfort; the
calm, beautiful Cecilia, surrounded by her bright
pretty children, whose individual developments

announced themselves at an early age, none showing any marked musical capacity. Felix himself was unceasingly employed, to my thinking, too continuously, not to awaken anxiety whether the nerves of his brain could hold out, which had been so strongly exerted from his earliest youth.

I came in for one Gewandhaus Concert, at which I heard the ninth symphony of Beethoven. Through Felix's conducting I understood the strange colossal work for the first time; so clearly detached and grouped were the masses, with such certainty was the enchainment of the phrases interpreted.

During these two days that I passed with Felix, I became clearly conscious of the change that had come over the sources of his inner life. His blooming youthful joyousness had given place to a fretfulness, a satiety of all earthly things, which reflected everything back differently from the spirit of former days.

His conducting of the concerts, everything that savoured of business, was an intolerable annoyance to him; the following winter he in-

tended to let Gade conduct the concerts entirely.
He took no longer any pleasure in the Conservatorium, he gave over the pianoforte pupils to
Moscheles; not one of the young people studying
compositions inspired him with any sympathy;
he crossly declared them all to be without talent,
and told me that he could not bear to see any
more of their compositions, that none of them
gave any hopes for the next generation of German
musicians.

The increasing industry, which had become his
second nature, incited him to be constantly composing. He called it "doing his duty;" but it
appeared to me, quite apart from considerations
of health, that he would have better fulfilled his
duty had he written less and waited for the happy
moments when his creative power was spontaneous, which did not come so often now as formerly. I had remarked lately that he began to
repeat himself in his composition; that he began,
unconsciously, to copy older masters, especially
Sebastian Bach, and that his writings exhibited
certain mannerisms. I told him these things,
and he received what I said without any irasci-

bility, because he believed me to be completely in error. He spoke disparagingly of ideas that had been waited for and contrived, and said that when one had at heart to compose music, the first involuntary thought would be the right one, even though it might not be so new or so striking, or though it might recall Sebastian Bach; if it did, it was a sign that so it was to have been.

It did not seem to me that the severe criticism he applied to his finished works, and his proneness to alter them, fitted in with these views; I thought he did not discriminate between his impulse to work and to create.

I have not been able to alter this opinion in the face of his later productions, even of "Elijah." Though this work contains beauties of the brightest period of the master, much in it seems to me laboured, and the labour is apparent; I miss the fresh current of imagination and feeling that flows so powerfully through "St. Paul." The "Fest-gesang" to Schiller's lines, "Der Menschheit Würde ist in eure Hand gegeben," which he pro-duced at the German-Flemish Musical Festival, in Whitsuntide of this year, also confirmed my opinion, when I heard it soon afterwards in Dresden, without the deceptive effect given to it by three thousand voices. I wished the more ardently that he might yet write an opera, and believed that in this little-trodden ground a new vein of his creative faculty would be opened. His fine and correct sense, his power of portraying character, promised the happiest results. We had again discussed the episode in the " Peasant's War," and, although I had already begun to be absorbed in my "History of Dramatic Art," I made a diversion, and began to put a plot together, and was in a position to write him details about the conduct of the story and the characters by the 13th of April, as also to assure him that his objection as to the similarity of the subject with that of " La Muette" was unfounded.

Meanwhile Felix had entered into communication with Geibel about the development of the " Loreley " subject, who spoke to me of it when on a visit to Dresden in April, and asked for my co-operation, which I willingly promised. Although this made my present labour of no use, I nevertheless sent it to Felix, to prove to him my willingness, but added, that I had better hopes of Geibel's work, which, to judge from his description, promised well; that this poet's beautiful and lyrical use of language removed all anxieties on that score, and that if he wished it, I would gladly help in the forming of the dramatic arrangement. To this he replied:

"Leipzig, May 9th, 1846.

"DEAR EDUARD,

"Thanks for your letter and the libretto, and above all for bearing me in mind so faithfully, and for the firm hope I now have that my long-standing wish will now at last be fulfilled, no less than for the many beautiful and good things contained in your sketch, which has greatly fascinated and attracted me.

"You wish that I should write you in detail about it, but, indeed, you have already felt and said in your letter all that I could suggest; you speak of 'some situations that would be effective, and which you are yet considering,' but I find so many excellent and effective ones already sketched out here, that I have no manner of doubt about those you have not yet put into shape.* The opening (let me say, by the way, almost the whole part of the peasant Catharine), nearly the whole of the second act, but above all the scene where Catharine goes off and he remains, and afterwards the countess appears, and the close of this act; the scene of the two men at the beginning of the third act, the drinking scene, where the count first comes on disguised as a monk,— all these are capital, admirable situations, so musical and so dramatic.

" You say that the action must be wound up differently; in any case it must remain tragical; this was your intention as well as mine. You mention two faults: 1. That there is yet too much historical ballast, and that the circumstances of the time in Galicia, its communism, are unfavourable elements. 2. That it does not yet impress you satisfactorily as a whole. To this I respond, if what you call historical ballast *can* be *lessened*, if some of these local matters *can* be

---

* The plot being unknown may render these comments somewhat obscure; to show the character of Mendelssohn's criticisms, however, I do not suppress them.

suppressed, then I think no fault will remain in
its construction; for these are the only points
that do not impress me favourably with the plot
as a whole—the number of allusions made to
freedom, bondage, and social conditions that run
through the whole. But can these be reduced?

"It would be most fortunate, indeed it is necessary, that these tendencies should play a less
prominent part. The very thing that would
make it desirable for some, local colouring, which
asserts itself so strongly just now, both on the
stage and in literature, would make it undesirable
to me. Where such colouring is *necessary*, why
not give it? then there should be no hesitating;
but where it is not necessary, for God's sake, let
us not have it, for thus it becomes the most
vicious hankering after effect, and ogling at the
public. So if you can throw away some of this
ballast here and there, as you say, it will be a
good thing on that account; besides we have had
too much of it these ten years; moreover, I
believe as you say, that this would most likely
be an impediment to the performance of the
opera; and, finally, several points, especially the

close of the first act, still remind me of ' La
Muette.'

" But with what subtleness the whole is managed,
I perceive, even in this. In the part of Catharine, too, the 'local tendencies' are continually
alluded to, but they never disturb me (except
perhaps in the tone of the first song) ; everything in her seems to me natural and necessary,
because all grows out of her character. As I
know that you have drawn the characters from
your own mind for this work, I am struck anew
with the conviction that such things are only
happy when they proceed from natural aptitude,
and no amount of talk or reasoning could make
them ; I hope this will be proved in the end.

" I would like to mention a few points that
pleased me less : for example, just after the scene
of the shooting contest ; another grows out of this
—that I think the brother of the countess too
obnoxious a fellow ; there is too little motive for
throwing Conrad into the tower ; also his be-
haviour at the end, in the monk's habit, when he
persuades the peasants to revolt, is too unsym-
pathetic.   As the piece is called ' Knight and

Peasant,' and must be so called from its subject, the knight should assert himself in contradistinction to the peasant differently from this, otherwise this very 'local tendency,' this *captatio benevolentiæ*, which we both like so little, will predominate and put us all out of humour.

"Give counsel!—the only thing that disturbs me in the second act is, that towards the end the countess becomes a little too didactic, or shall you pass briefly over some of the points that I mention here? for, at that moment of the action, in the midst of so much excitement, she must not give so much importance to the inequality of the marriage. What do you say to this? say it soon; and write me soon again.

"And you will also assist Geibel in his poem? What a good and kind friend you are! Do you like what he has done so far? but above all things let nothing hinder you in working out your own ideas, otherwise the end of all will be that I get neither one or other of the poems, and I do so long to have one of them completed soon, and two would be still better.

"Now write me soon again; remember me to

your household. Farewell, and receive a thousand
hearty thanks from your

"FELIX M.-B."

Any further time spent upon my plot appeared
to me would be wasted ; to treat an episode in
the "Peasant's War" without bringing in the
conditions of the period, I did not think feasible.
I considered Geibel's work much more likely,
and was ready with pleasure to help him in it.
I soon saw, however, that the poet was far from
having as yet brought the subject into the concise
limits requisite for musical treatment ; his ideas
seemed all to assume the form of song or romance.
As I had already thought through the subject, I
was enabled to make various suggestions, and so
the leading incidents were grouped into three
acts, in the last of which only a change of scene
was indispensable : I had the best expectations
of the success of the work. When Geibel brought
me the first act a fortnight afterwards, which I
found beautifully and poetically indited, but not
at all rounded off into operatic shape, I saw that
Mendelssohn himself must be consulted, before

further proceeding would be of any use. I wrote
to him on the 14th of May,—that it would be a
thousand pities, if this work did not turn out to be
something good, and that, therefore, everything
must be done to make his first real opera all that
it could be. I added, "Geibel thinks that some
of my propositions are not in accordance with
your wishes, but I believe he cannot have understood you. If he is to proceed in making you an
available work, you must distinctly agree with
him about the distribution of the scenes, action,
position, and nature of the pieces of music, otherwise you will be playing at cross purposes for
months yet, before the work receives any tangible
shape. Geibel thought of going to you to Leipzig,
but there is much he will not be able to justify to
you and explain, because he has as yet too little
experience in this kind of work ; besides he is apt
to waver, and, from modesty, easily yields. It
appears to me very desirable, for the sake of the
work, that you should come for a day to Dresden.
If you would like to discuss and fix the development of the plot, in my presence, my experience
will enable me, at once, to explain to you the

practical working of each point; we will settle exactly how it is to be, and then Geibel, aided by my advice, can work out the literary part until it is ready for you. You have confidence in me in such things," I concluded, " do what I ask. Come, otherwise the work cannot proceed reliably."

Felix replied the following day.

"Leipzig, the 15th May, 1846.

" DEAR EDUARD,

"Thousand thanks for your letter, but it is a sheer impossibility that I should go to Dresden during these days, for this day week I must start for the Rhine festivals, and first I must complete the greater part of my new oratorio, at which I am working day and night to send to England, otherwise it will not be in time. So I have not an hour to lose. Besides, my presence there would be of very little use; I have thought the matter over and over, and I can do nothing to improve it,—my *ressort* will begin again (as we are of one mind about the subject, and the division of the action) with the score. I shall be satisfied with *everything*, so that it is *truly dramatic*. Whatever is truly dramatic I shall be able to set to music, and for this reason I should prefer that *no* wishes of mine should be taken into account, but that you and Geibel should do what you think right and fitting, without reference to anything else. I only beg of you to continue in your kind and friendly disposition towards the work,—how much I am thankful to you, I am sure you know. I can scarcely find time for these lines, all my thoughts are in my score. Thanks! thanks! Thou true, good, and faithful friend! Thy

" FELIX."

This was the last letter I received from him.

I regretted that he could not come to us, regretted that his old repugnance to plod carefully through a subject with others should influence this work; I sought as much as I could to look to his interest in the affair, not without apprehension that he would afterwards find much to disapprove of.

Geibel was advanced into the second act; I had good hopes the poem would turn out well, when he was summoned to Karlsbad by Kugler, who was staying there. He fancied he thoroughly understood my views about the second, and more difficult half, and quitted Dresden. Felix went to the musical festivals on the Rhine, and back again to Leipzig, to finish "Elijah," which he produced at Birmingham in August with immense success.

On his return to Leipzig he sought as much as possible to free himself from public duties. His lassitude increased, or rather his irascible repugnance to the turmoil of life; whoever did not truly know him might suppose that he had grown proud. We saw him in Dresden on the 17th of November, whither he had brought Cecilia and some relations from Frankfort to enjoy the picture gallery, which Cecilia did not yet know. We met often, both at our respective houses and at friends'; he took great interest in my reading of "Minna von Barnhelm," and in a conversation about it he showed a most intimate acquaintance with the poem, which he prized highly, even to

pointing out little features of it, seldom noticed.
All friends in Dresden, however, were struck by
his excessive touchiness, which approached the
quarrelsome testiness of his father. He was particularly annoyed by the political ferment of the
day, and predicted evil of it from every one of its
exaggerations, which were certainly numerous
enough. He who had in his youth been a declared radical, who had gloried only five years
ago in Jakoby's "Vier Fragen,"* in an ecstasy
of patriotism, he was now deeply hurt and
agitated by the results of those harbingers of
freedom. Because he disapproved of the leaders,
he disapproved of the movement; he wished that
the ameliorations should be effected by lawful
authority. Thus he wanted the establishment of
the Protestant religion in Saxony, which at that
time agitated the public mind, should be removed
from the jurisdiction of the Landtag, and of the
congregations, to that of the clergy, whose business
it was; and he was offended when I asked him

* "The Four Questions," a powerful pamphlet that appeared on the accession of Frederic William IV., expressing
the nation's apprehensions lest the king should repudiate the
promised political reforms, as his father had done.—TR.

whether he had become a Roman Catholic, and
acknowledged no longer our universal priesthood.

It was evident that he was under the dominion
of an irritation of the nerves of the brain, which
led him to avert all commotion in his thoughts
as he would have averted noise when at his work.

Apart from this weakness, his manner of thinking and feeling, his pure humanity was as sound
and strong as in his freshest time. I would recall
the letter to Moscheles of June 26, 1846, in which
he so energetically protests against the dismissal
of two English orchestra players, who had behaved unbecomingly towards him at a Philharmonic concert, and whom the committee of the
Birmingham Festival intended to punish by ex-
cluding them.

Felix and Cecilia recounted to us about their
servant Johann, who had fallen ill in October,
and of the troubles they had to induce their
doctor to treat the worthy fellow with sufficient
care. The doctor required that he should be sent
to the hospital, as he had not time to attend upon
servants in prolonged illness. Upon this Felix
had declared that he insisted upon the faithful

fellow-being nursed in his house, that he was as much a member of his household as any one else, and that to refuse him medical attendance was to refuse it to his household. This helped. The patient himself, however, sorely put the kind indulgence of his masters to the test. As he had been the *factotum* of the house, he persisted in arranging, and being told of everything still, from his sick bed. His bell was incessantly in motion, wanting to know what was passing; indeed Cecilia told us, during a dinner-party which gave the other servants enough to do to supply his place and their own, he was perpetually ringing, in order to be told which guests had arrived, who had carried in such or such a dish, and how it had been put on the table. "I had to sit down at his bed-side," concluded Cecilia, "to tell him everything circumstantially." The Mendelssohns related all this with laughter, as one would overlook the naughtiness of a sick child. They then expected that he would recover; their disappointment in this, and the shock that the death of this worthy fellow gave to Felix, is told in his letter to Klingemann of the 6th of December.

The remainder of the winter Felix passed in composition, undisturbed by concert business. He was preparing a new oratorio, "Christus." Once more he came to Dresden on the 27th of February, 1847, to a court concert. With an air of resignation he presented Geibel's poem of "Loreley" to me, which he had just received. "There it is," he said; "look at it; and do not again call me obstinate and contrary when I tell you that, as it is, I cannot set it to music."

I certainly found that it had not been worked out so well as I had expected; I was obliged to confess to him next day that it could not remain in its present shape. We now deliberated how it was to be mended, and it could not be denied that, had we met and discussed the matter at the beginning, all the difficulties that were now before us might have been saved. Felix returned home much out of humour about his constant ill fate wherever operas were concerned.

This was the last time we spoke to each other. The wish he had harboured ever since the Berlin excitements, to live quietly and comfortably in the midst of his family and old friends, was now much in his thoughts. He intended to spend the summer in Frankfort, to build a house there, and to winter in Berlin, amongst his relatives. The letter to his brother-in-law, Dirichlet, of January 4, 1847, persuading him not to leave Berlin, shows how painfully anxious he was that none should part out of the circle in which he wished to live.

In the spring he again went to England, witnessed the triumphs of his " Elijah," conducted the music of his " Midsummer-Night's Dream " at a Philharmonic concert, and there played the G major concerto of Beethoven with enthusiastic applause. After this visit he returned to Frankfort, where he met his wife and children, and intended to pass the summer happily with them ; and here the terrible blow fell upon him, like a stroke of lightning from an unclouded sky, of the sudden death of his sister Fanny.

In perfect health and cheerfulness she had been presiding at a vocal rehearsal for the next of her Sunday performances, on the afternoon of May the 14th. All at once she felt her hands powerless on the keys, and was compelled to ask a friend to take her place at the instrument. The rehearsal proceeded; it was of the choruses of the "Walpurgis Night;" she was listening to them from an inner room, through the open doors, whilst she was fomenting her hands in hot vinegar. "How beautiful it sounds!" she said, joyfully; she thought herself restored, and was on the point of returning to the music-room, when a second and total paralysis struck her; she lost consciousness, and had breathed her last by eleven o'clock that night.

The death of this rare woman was felt in a very wide circle, and the nearer were the ties that bound others to her, the more irretrievable they felt her loss to be. A character so fully, not only under the dominion, but thoroughly penetrated by intellect and a lofty sense of right, which preserved the balance of every faculty and power, and left no room for any pettiness of vanity or envy,—of such a character there can never be many instances; and such a character could not but exert a deep and beneficial influence upon all who were dear to her. And upon Felix her loss fell heavier than upon any one, bound up with her as he was in all his musical associations from earliest childhood. To his grief was also

added the terrible presentiment, which he had
conceived already at his mother's death, that,
judging from the sudden death of his father and
grandfather and her own, he believed that cerebral paralysis must be a family doom : this presentiment was now confirmed by the death of his
beloved sister. Henceforth he lived as under the
impending sword of the Angel of Death, and
longed more and more to seclude himself in domestic life.

He went with his family to Baden-Baden, where
his brother joined them, and then to Interlaken,
of which he was so fond. His letters, written in
August, describe his retired life there amidst his
wife and children.

He did not give up work, however, as though
he must be doing whilst it was yet day. He
was not only busy with the oratorio " Christus,"
but went at the opera " Loreley," although the
libretto was yet far from satisfying him. He
hoped it would yet assume the shape he wished ;
he was anxious to keep his word with Jenny
Lind ; to complete the opera was his earnest
desire. And so he sketched out several pieces

for it, completed the finale to the first act, which has become known both on the stage and in the concert-room, and proves how much the world has lost through Mendelssohn's critical fastidiousness, which doomed his brightest powers to inactivity. There is a Hamlet-like tragedy about Mendelssohn's operatic destiny. During eighteen years he could not make up his mind firmly to adopt any subject and work it out, because he wanted perfection; and when at last he overcame his scruples and determined upon a poem, though far from what it should have been, he sank with his fragment into the grave.

Returned to Leipzig in September, he paid a short visit to his relatives in Berlin at the end of this month; here he pledged himself to perform several times during the coming winter; he had also engaged himself to conduct his "Elijah" in Vienna during November, and had appointed to meet Geibel to discuss the alterations of the "Loreley" libretto. But on the 25th of October, in Leipzig, where he was overwhelmed with work, he had the first attack of acute headache. No

danger was yet thought of, the pain left him ; he
still contemplated the visit to Vienna, and intended to meet Geibel on the road to Berlin, at
Jüterbogk, to settle upon the catastrophe of the
" Loreley :" the opera was the last care of his
life.

In Dresden we only knew that Mendelssohn
had been unwell, but on the 2nd of November we
heard that he had had a relapse, that he was
mostly in a state of unconsciousness, that the
doctors were in fear ;—and so were we.   Under
these circumstances I heard " Elijah " for the first
time on the 3rd by the Singakademie in Dresden.
What was more natural than that in the over-
whelming impression I received from the music of
my friend—which at all times sounded to me as
though it proceeded from my own soul—I should
hear, beyond the clear and masterly ideas, the
fine part-writing and instrumentation, the sweet
comforting voices of the angels, the scene of healing the sick son, and the flight to heaven, the
breath of the great master hovering between life
and death, and already consecrated to a higher
existence ?

On the following day the news were contradic-
tory, the next again they were bad. The blessing
of telegraphic messages was not yet known. On
the 5th I went in the evening to Bendemann,
where I hoped to learn the latest tidings
from Leipzig; there came Clara Schumann with
a letter, weeping;—Felix had died yesterday
evening, November the 4th!

He was the youngest of my friends, but our
friendship was the oldest.

The following morning I went with the Dresden
friends to Leipzig, to accompany Felix on his
last journey. His brother, who had been called
from Berlin when he was struck the second time,
on the 30th October, recounted to me what happened during the last days.

On the 3rd Felix had spoken cheerfully with
him for hours, until midday, then he became restless, and Paul and Cecilia were in alternate attendance at his bedside. Towards two o'clock
Cecilia came in terror to call Paul, as she could
not soothe the patient. Paul went in to him,
scolded him in jest, which Felix was yet able to
understand and respond to. But suddenly he

started up, as though seized with a frightful pain
in his head, his mouth open with an agonizing
expression; he gave one piercing cry and sank
back upon his pillow.   Now all was over ;   from
this time he lay in a dull half-sleep, answered
only " Yes," and " No ;" and only once to Cecilia's
tender inquiry, how he felt? answered "Tired,
very tired !" Thus he dozed quietly until twenty-
four minutes past nine, when his breathing ceased
and life was extinct.

Hensel, whom I met again now, and who was
still quite crushed by the death of his wife, led
me to the corpse, which he had thoughtfully
decorated.   There lay my beloved friend, in a
costly coffin, upon cushions of satin, embowered
in tall growing shrubs, and covered with wreaths
of flowers and laurels.   He looked much aged,
but recalled to me the expression of the boy as I
had first seen him ;—where my hand had so often
stroked the long brown locks and the burning
brow, I now touched the marble forehead of the
man.   This span of time in my remembrance
encloses the whole of happy youth, in one perfect
and indelible thought.

Cecilia sent for me the following morning; she received me with the tenderness of a sister, wept in silence, and was calm and composed as ever.

She thanked me for all the love and devotion I had shown to her Felix, grieved for me that I should have to mourn so faithful a friend, and spoke of the love with which Felix had always regarded me. Long we spoke of him, it comforted her, and she was loth for me to depart. She was most unpretending in her sorrow, gentle, and resigned to live for the care and education of her children. She said, "God would help her, and surely her boys would have the inheritance of some of their father's goodness."

There could not be a more worthy memorial of him than the well-balanced, strong and tender heart of his mourning widow.

In the afternoon the immense throng of the funeral procession began to gather in front of the house, and was put in motion about four o'clock. The coffin was covered with a rich funeral pall of velvet embroidered in silver, and thickly set round with the customary offering in Leipzig of palm branches, of which there was a gigantic array round the sarcophagus, that gave it the aspect of an isle of peace in the midst of the surging crowd. Streets and open places were all filled with people ; all the windows were crowded on the long and circuitous road that the procession was to pass, through the town and by the Gewandhaus, the scene of Mendelssohn's labours. The musicians led the way, playing a hastily-instrumented song without words by Mendelssohn ;* six clergymen in full robes followed the bier, then came the relatives, the heads of the musical societies, then his friends, of whom many had arrived in the course of the day from a distance, led by Schubring and myself. A second division followed, preceded by clergymen ; night was closing in when we arrived at the church of the University. The coffin was put down, by accident, close to where I stood ; the palm branches rustled in my face ; it seemed to me as though the departed whispered to me, " I leave my peace with you !"

The procession was received at the church with the music in " Antigone " that accompanies the

---

* The one in E minor, Book 5.

corpse of Hœmon. The acute shake in it reminded me of a word Felix said to me when he
was a boy, how he had met a military funeral
procession, and that the music had begun with a
high shake, which had appeared to him to convey
an expression of sharp anguish. And thus he
had applied it long years afterwards in " Antigone," and thus it did express the sharpness of
anguish to those who accompanied his last earthly
journey.

During the choral, " Jesus meine Zuversicht,"
the bier was placed upon a raised platform in
the choir, with six high candelabra beside it, and
at the end of the lighted church, below the organ,
there loomed the orchestra, densely filled with
musicians and singers. We heard choruses from
" St. Paul," a discourse of Pastor Howard,
then the final chorus of Bach's " Passion," " Wir
setzten uns mit Thränen nieder," &c., " Ruhe,
sanfte Ruhe,"* and thus our mourning rites were
brought to a close.

When the church was almost deserted, a female
form, in deep mourning, was led to the bier ; she

* " We sat down in tears."   " Rest, gentle rest."

sank down beside it, and remained long in prayer. It was Cecilia, taking her last farewell of the earthly remains of Felix; she knew that she would not long survive him.

The corpse was taken the same night by special train to Berlin, being received on its road with a pious tribute of song, by the vocal societies, at Cöthen and at Dessau. Arrived at Berlin, it was placed in the family vault, side by side with Fanny's remains, during a performance of Beethoven's " Funeral March," under Taubert's direction, singing of the Domchor and of the Singakademie, and a discourse by Pastor Berduschek.

When Felix parted for the last time from Fanny she reproached him, that he had not for so many years spent her birthday with her; as he stepped into the carriage he took her hand, and said, " Depend upon it, the next I shall spend with you!" He kept his word, for Fanny's birthday was on the 8th of November.*

---

* It would seem a pity to disturb the impression of completeness left by this coincidence, were not truth better than all. Mendelssohn's letters to his sister Fanny, of November

Mendelssohn's death has almost universally
been bewailed as a premature one; that I should
so have lamented it will seem natural—what did
I not lose in him? what hopes had I not rested
on him? But when the stroke of death had
fallen, I was taught that this parting whilst life
is at its height was best, and harmonized with
his singularly favoured destiny.

So richly favoured and endowed, so beloved
and admired, and at the same time so strong in
mind and character, that he never once let slip
the bridle of religious discipline, nor the just
sense of modesty and humility, nor ever fell short
of his standard of duty. Earth denied him none
of her joys, and Heaven granted him the fulfilment of all the wishes of his heart. How little
in this great circumference of peace and happiness seem the hours of querulous humours, the
days of vexation, and those of mortal discomfort
at the false honours that were heaped upon
him! In the midst of work newly begun, of

16, 1830, and of November 14, 1834 and 1840, state the latter
date to have been that of her birthday, as does also the inscription on her tombstone.—Tr.

far-reaching intentions, the rapid death that removed him from our world of anxiety and
uncertainty completed the brilliant career of a
man who was called into life truly for his own
and others' happiness.

INDEX.

———◆◇◆———

X

THE END.

DATE DUE

DATE DUE			
JAN 16 75			
GAYLORD			PRINTED IN U.S.A.